Reconciliation
between
God and Man

By

W. J. Sparrow-Simpson, D.D.,

Chaplain of S. Mary's Hospital, Ilford.

Society for Promoting Christian Knowledge
LONDON: NORTHUMBERLAND AVENUE, W.C.
BRIGHTON: 129 NORTH STREET
1916

Contents

The Incarnation:
God in Christ

The Incarnation:
God in Christ

"God was in Christ reconciling the world unto Himself,"
2 Cor. v. 19.

THAT in some sense or other GOD was in
CHRIST most religious people will admit.
The difficulty is in what sense the words are to be
understood. GOD was in CHRIST. Can anything
be more plain ? Yet it covers a multitude of
meanings. It can be made to mean so much, or
else so little. It is a convenient expression for
those who are satisfied to argue in words, while
they differ about realities. The Churchman can
say it, and the Unitarian can say it. But what
the one denotes the other denies. What we want
to notice is the true relation between GOD and
CHRIST. The simplest way to understand it is to
compare it with certain other phrases.

I

FIRST then we say that God is in Nature.
1. The theory of the relation of God to Nature
held by the Deists of the Eighteenth Century
was that God and Nature were entirely separate.
God was supposed to have called Nature into
being, to have handed it over to the management
of a company of forces called the laws of Nature,
while He Himself resided at an immeasurable
distance away from its machinery, with which
He could not be expected to interfere. God's

B 2

work was supposed to exist independently of its Maker much in the same way as the work of a man survives the maker's departure or forgetfulness or decease.

2. Exactly opposed to this was the theory of the Pantheist. God and Nature, said the Pantheist, are identified. God is the underlying reality, the impersonal substratum of all appearances. Nature denotes the phenomena which arise out of God, and fall back again into the immensity from which they spring.

3. Now Christianity blends together these opposite ideas. It affirms that both these theories contain large elements of truth. The Pantheist is perfectly right when he says that God and Nature are inseparable. God pervades all Nature through and through. He is present in every beast, in every blade of grass, in every atom. S. Paul adopts the Pantheist expression 'in Him we live and move and have our being.' Herein lies the difference between the work of God and the work of man. Man works from without, God from within. Man can depart and forget his work and it exists without him. But if God withdrew for a single instant from His work it would instantly sink back into nothingness and cease entirely to exist. The presence of God in Nature is the indispensable condition of its being.

On the other hand the Deist is perfectly right when he says that God and Nature cannot be identified. For God is spirit, is personal, and spirit cannot be identified with matter, nor that which is personal with that which is not. God then is distinct from Nature and its superior.

4

Two phrases are required to describe the relation in which God stands to Nature. One is Divine Immanence, for God pervades all Nature through and through. The other is Divine Transcendence, for God surpasses Nature as widely as moral personality surpasses the non-moral and the impersonal.

When therefore we say that God is in Nature, what we mean is this : the self-existent personality pervades all Nature by His creative and sustaining power.

II

Secondly, there is another familiar expression to be considered. For as we commonly say that God is in Nature, so again we say that God is in mankind. We say that God is in the hearts of good men.

Now God is in mankind in a higher sense from that in which He is in Nature. For this is a relation between Persons : a moral relationship. The presence of God in Nature is one which cannot be cast out except at the price of ceasing to exist. But the presence of God in the human heart can be cast out altogether, while physical existence endures. God's sustaining presence can remain while His moral presence is withdrawn. His sustaining presence enables the human will to do what of necessity He must condemn.

The presence of God in man exists in endlessly various degrees. It may not be exactly the same in any two of us. Certainly the presence of God in Judas was a very different degree from the presence of God in S. John. The heart of man is designed to be the Temple of God, the place for the Divine indwelling. God may be in you of a truth.

But this presence of God in man, however intimate and profound, is still a relation between a person who is Divine and a person who is human ; between an uncreated personality and a created one. And the human never becomes Divine. It is impossible for the human to be elevated into Deity. The abyss between created and uncreated can never be surpassed to the extent that one who began existence as human completes it by becoming Divine.

The proof of this is plain. We come near to the Divine in the saint. But the saint can never become the object of our worship, our adoration. In spite of the Divine indwelling in man we cannot ascribe to the man the attributes of Deity.

III

We now come to the language of the text : God was in Christ. This is in a sense quite different from those considered hitherto. God was not in Christ merely in the same sense in which He is in every good man. For example, God was not in Christ merely in the same sense in which He was in S. John. Christ is not S. John's superior through an intensified infusion of grace. The difference between the two is not that the one had much grace and the other had more, so that if the grace bestowed upon S. John had been indefinitely increased he would literally have become another Christ, our Lord's equal in every respect. Saints are not potential Christs. Heaven will not exhibit a countless multitude of Christs. There is only one Christ, and there never will be more than one.

What then is meant by the phrase God is in Christ? The meaning, according to the Church, is expressed by the term Incarnation. According to the fourth Evangelist it is explained by saying, ' In the beginning was the Word, and the Word was with God, and the Word was God. . . . And the Word became flesh and dwelt among us.'

IV

What then does Incarnation mean?

Incarnation presupposes distinctions within the Divine personality. It requires the belief that the Fatherhood of God denotes before all things else His relationship to the Eternal Son. And the doctrine of Incarnation is this: that the Eternal Son of God entered into human history. He consented to live under human conditions. He experienced what it is to be a man; He reduced Himself to life under human limitations. He took to Himself the constituents of our mortal nature. He Who is the All-wise took to Himself a human mind, passed through the successive stages of infancy, childhood, youth and maturity, submitting to know nothing but what it should please the Father to declare to Him, and what He should ascertain by purely human means. He grew in wisdom as He grew in stature. He looked out on the world with a human mind. He thought and spoke as a man, and in the language of men.

7

He lived a purely human life of submission and dependence upon the Father in Heaven. He, the All-powerful, took a human will. He did nothing but what a human will aided by the Father could do.

V

Incarnation is *not the adoption by a Divine Person of a human individual.* It does not mean that the Son of God was related to the son of Mary in the same way that He was to the sons of Zebedee. It does not mean that the Son of God stood more closely related to the son of Mary than to other women's sons, because of the exceptional excellence of His character, or the peculiar endowments with which He was graced. The Son of God was related to the sons of Zebedee as one person is related with other persons. Their minds were their own, not His. Their wills were theirs, not His. But the Son of God was not related to the son of Mary as one person is to another. *They were identified.* They were one and the same. The personality of the Son of God was the personality of the son of Mary. The human mind of Jesus was the property of the Son of God.

Incarnation then means that the same individual being is perfect God and perfect man.

VI

Incarnation then is Divine Personality experiencing what it is to be man.

THE INCARNATION : GOD IN CHRIST

Such a doctrine is in reality *unique* among the religions of the world. We sometimes hear of an Indian doctrine of Reincarnation. But that is an entirely different thing. The Indian means that a human soul after it leaves the body reappears in another form, sometimes human, sometimes merely animal, taking another body for a time, and entering perhaps into a whole succession of bodies one after another. But this is strictly nothing more than re-embodiment. It is not in the least what is meant by Incarnation.

It is of the essence of Incarnation that the person incarnate is Divine, and that He takes to Himself the entire constituents of human nature, body, mind, heart and will, and that He is identified with the humanity which He has assumed for ever. In the very nature of the case Incarnation can only happen once.

Yet at the same time, while the Incarnation is unique it *completes a process*. It is not isolated from all the previous dealings of God with His creatures. It is not as if God were up to that time entirely separate from the creation and suddenly entered into it. On the contrary. God was already in Nature by His sustaining power. He was already in Mankind by moral influence and grace. But these inferior stages of Divine relation to the Universe were now consummated in a yet more wondrous and sublime relationship. God now became, personally in Christ, incarnate on the earth.

Difficulties presented by the Incarnation

Difficulties presented by the Incarnation

" How can these things be ? " St. John iii. 9.

INCARNATION means the Divine Personality experiencing life under human conditions. It means that the eternally pre-existing Son of God took to Himself the constituent elements of humanity and reduced His wisdom to the limits of His human mind.

Now, beyond all question this is a stupendous idea. No wonder if it raises doubts and difficulties. No wonder if thoughtful men and women ask the Church, as Nicodemus asked Christ, ' How can these things be ? '

Let us consider, then, some of the difficulties which this central Christian doctrine awakens in the modern mind. We believe this doctrine to be profoundly true. But it would be a fatal policy to ignore in church what is being said outside. These difficulties exist as obstacles to faith. You are liable to be challenged by them at any time. We ought, therefore, to consider them, not so much for our own sake as for the sake of those who stand without, and who, but for these difficulties, would be perhaps within.

I

One difficulty raised against the Incarnation is that the world is too insignificant for such a doctrine to be true. A Unitarian writer says that he should like to be informed why this tiny sphere was selected as the scene for so amazing a miracle.[1] He is deeply impressed by the insignificance of the earth relatively to boundless space. Such a selection on the part of Deity seems to him impossible to credit.

Now, in reply, it may fairly be said that the idea of human insignificance is hardly new in the history of religious thought. It was keenly felt two thousand years ago and more ; and the Psalmist has framed the experience for all time in memorable words.[2]

There is no novelty in the experience. Which of us has not at some time or other felt the overwhelming sense of the insignificance of the world in contrast with the starry heights ? The only question is what is the true interpretation of this experience ?

Let us consider now the difficulty in four different aspects : As it concerns religion ; as it concerns space ; as it concerns the human mind ; and as it concerns God.

1. First then, as it concerns Religion.

I do not understand how a religious man can urge the insignificance of the earth as an argument against the Incarnation. For, if that argument has any real weight, it cuts at the very root of all religion and of all belief in the providence of God. A sceptical writer has shown this in the clearest way. He says that when the earth was regarded as the established centre of

---

[1] Drummond, *Christian Doctrine*, p. 278.
[2] Ps. viii.

all the worlds, while sun and moon and stars did obeisance circling round it, the importance of the earth's inhabitants seemed to follow easily as a matter of course. But now that science has reversed all this, and demonstrates the earth to be nothing better than a third-rate satellite of an inferior sun, mankind is correspondingly reduced in value. The human race is seen to be purely suburban, living obviously on the fringes of the huge metropolis of existence. As for the notion of its immortality, that is simply preposterous, a mere product of exaggerated self-esteem, due to nothing more than what the author calls 'man's egotistical religiosity.' In view of the boundless immensity of worlds, it is 'no longer possible to assign supreme importance to man's intelligence or to spiritual valuations.'

Now there is one thing to be said in favour of this sceptical view. It is, at any rate, thoroughgoing and consistent. Grant him his premisses, and he does not shrink from their logical conclusion.

And what I would desire to do is to leave the Unitarian to answer him. For the Unitarian, while deeply impressed by the earth's insignificance, does not consider that insignificance to be any argument whatever against the providential government of the world, or against the individual immortality of man. Let him therefore give the sceptic his reasons for this belief, and he will find that in so doing he has refuted his own objection to the Incarnation. For, if the insignificance of the earth does not carry with it the insignificance of the earth's inhabitants, then neither can it be any argument against the Incarnation.

2. Secondly, let us consider the subject of Space.

Man, instructed by modern science, lifts up his eyes to the heavens and then looks upon the earth beneath, and the contrast overwhelms him. Far out, in all directions of the boundless waste, are worlds and systems of worlds, with hints of immensities beyond, until the transient inhabitant of the earth, confounded before these bewildering magnitudes, is constrained to cry, ' Man is like a thing of naught.'

Nevertheless, while there is the immeasurably vast, there is also the immeasurably little. For, as numbers can be indefinitely increased, so also they can be indefinitely diminished. If there is a positive extension to infinity, there is a negative shrinking to infinity also. From the earth we may take a descending scale of magnitudes, to the smallest insect, to the parasite on a gnat's wing, to the smallest of its veins, to a single drop of blood within that vein, then less and less, by a process of continuous diminution, to the atom itself, which is too infinitesimal to be verified by the senses, and can only be reached at all by a process of inference.[1] The atom for science was, until recently, the ultimate. But this atom itself, by definition indivisible, and once concluded ultimate, is now resolvable into a vast system of elements moving with speed terrific within limits too inconceivably infinitesimal even

[1] Galloway, *Principles of Religious Development*, p. 262.

to be reached by our imaginations. Here, then, is the immeasurably small.[1]

It is as Pascal said, centuries ago : ' Man stands between two immensities : the immeasurably vast and the immeasurably little.' If, then, man is reduced to spacial nothingness relatively to the boundlessly vast, he is restored to spacial dignity relatively to the boundlessly little. And if the vast impresses us more than the little, that is far more due to our imagination than it is to our reason. For, strictly speaking, the one is just as real as the other.

3. Thirdly, let us consider the human mind.

Men look out upon the distant universe. They try to take its measurements. They are deeply impressed by its property of boundless extent. Then they infer that value must be measured in terms of space. And then they conclude the insignificance of mankind. But they have made the strangest of all omissions. They have confined attention to the object seen. But they have ignored the self or seer by whom the object is beheld. And yet the whole conception of size or space is clearly relative to the mind which reflects. Is not the whole idea of space a pure creation of the mind ? It would puzzle the wisest to say what is the meaning of a relation without a mind to relate it. There would be no problem at all were it not for the existence of mind.

The mind's assertion of its own insignificance confronting space is really a case of mock humility. How can the mind declare that that which is relative to mind is mind's superior ? Surely the

[1] Ladd, *Knowledge, Life, and Reality,* p. 202.

proper inference is not, How important a thing is space! but rather, How wondrous a thing is mind, which can create out of the unconscious universe such problems and such questionings as these!

4. Finally, let us attempt to consider the subject from the side of God. Let us try to realise God's estimate of worth. No doubt size is impressive to human beings; but this is because they are human, and themselves related to space. But is it credible that space impresses God in the same way that it does a man? A planet or a system of stars cannot be more impressive to God than a gnat or an atom. A million miles of space cannot affect the Divine imagination more forcibly than the millionth part of an inch. Is God Himself exceedingly vast, or is He excessively little? He is neither; for He is Spirit. He does not take valuations in the style of a quantity surveyor, estimating values at so much a square yard and so much a ton. As heaven is distant from earth, so are His thoughts higher than our thoughts, and His ways than our ways. God is personal; God is moral. These are His deepest characteristics, His real self. What He values most must be the personal and the moral, because with them He has the profoundest affinities. And valuing the personal and the moral most, who can say what sacrifices He may not make, what methods He may employ to protect or develop or perfect that type of existence which He values most? Consequently, the supposition that God could not have become incarnate on earth because the earth is small, is

an objection founded on the blunder that God's thoughts are ours. It is in reality a purely provincial and anthropomorphic view, which in the presence of ampler ideas of Deity is bound to disappear.

Tried, then, by these four great tests, its bearing on religion, on space, on mind, and on God, this objection to the Incarnation seems shattered into pieces.

II

So far, then, for the difficulty concerning space. Secondly, there arises another difficulty, that concerning time. The same Unitarian writer already quoted says that he should like to be informed why, if the Incarnation was true, it was for so many ages delayed. The greater its importance the sooner it ought to have come about. Why should countless thousands of human beings have died before this essential fact was achieved ?

Now, in reply to this, suppose we were compelled to answer, ' I really do not know, I cannot tell,' would our inability to answer prove that the Incarnation never happened ? Does human incapacity to explain the doings of the Most High demonstrate that the doings are not His ? Or can we not credit God with power to carry out plans which baffle our power to comprehend ? Are we not, as a fact, surrounded by many things which are as undeniably God's doing as they are to us impossible to explain ? Even then, if we had to answer, ' We cannot tell why Incarnation should have been so long delayed,' our incompetence would not necessarily cast any shadow of doubt upon the question whether it was true.

But we are not really in this position. It is possible for us, I believe, to give a satisfying reason why the Incarnation only happened after the lapse of many human centuries.

The further we go back in the life of man the more crude and imperfect does his religion become. Far back in the dawn of intelligence came the belief in innumerable deities, personifications of the forces of Nature, with attributes for the most part divorced from morality. Then in the civilised and cultured world arose the natural reaction. Men derided in private what they worshipped in public, and said that such religion was good enough for the masses, but not good enough for them. Instead of believing in many deities, they preferred the theory that there was no God at all. In sheer negation the human mind could never rest. Another idea arose. Yes, God exists ; or rather there are two, and one of them is good and the other is evil ; and the conflict of these antagonistic principles accounts for the mingled good and evil in mankind. That doctrine also slowly failed. And then at length, after many struggles and great difficulties, there arose, on the soil of Palestine and in the heart of Israel, that glorious and sublime conception that God is one and God is holy, which for all time lies at the basis of all true religion.

Now, if this represents at all accurately the outline of religious growth, we may well ask ourselves the question, Where in all this process could Incarnation have taken place ? For Incarnation obviously requires conditions. A perfect human life (that is to say, a human life capable of becoming the ideal for all ages because it is in possession of true religion and true morality) cannot conceivably be matured and developed except in an environment where very high religious and moral conditions already exist.

Two requisites for a perfect human life are these : first a nation and then a home wherein such a life might reasonably expand. Incarnation of the Divine in the human presupposes an arena furnished with religious ideas and principles and practices of such a kind that the Divine under human conditions can accept them as His own.

There were three conspicuous nations in the time of Christ : there was the Roman, with his genius for practical and military organisation; there was the Greek, with his depth of thought, his æsthetic tastes, his unrivalled mastery of art and eloquence ; and there was the little Semitic nation between the Jordan and the inland sea, conspicuous neither for empire nor for intellect, but with its own peculiar genius for religion, unique in sublimity and intensity. There were three conspicuous nations and three great cities : Rome, Athens, and Jerusalem. In which of these was Incarnation possible ? Could the Son of God be born in Rome or in Athens ? Could He be entrusted as a child to some Greek woman believer in the pagan deities ? Could He dwell in a city which, with all its æsthetic beauty, roused the moral indignation of S. Paul when he saw it wholly given over to a debased idolatry ? Could

He share the worship in the temple of Venus
or Apollo ?

Will it be said that the Divine, if incarnate,
could surely transcend His human environment ?
But if He did, it would not be a normal growth.
It would be the life of a child perpetually in conflict with His home on earth in order to be true
to His home in heaven. It would be an absolutely
abnormal condition, an unthinkable condition
every way. It would be altogether an unexemplary
childhood ; anything rather than the childhood
of an ideal human career.

Clearly, then, there was only one people within
which Incarnation could occur. It was the people
of Israel. And for that purpose there had to be
an age-long preparation. Jerusalem must first be
built. The Temple must be raised, and the offering
must first be presented. The great conception of
God, the ethical monotheism of Israel, must first
sink down into the nation's heart, the Psalms must
first be written in order that the Incarnate One
should find ideas and truths and worship of the
heavenly Father all prepared for Him to make
His human experience possible. And within the
nation must be the woman, the woman chosen
out of all womankind to be the mother of the
Incarnate Son.

Accordingly, when S. Paul says that it was
' when the fulness of the time was come ' that
God sent forth His Son, he says what commends
itself to common sense, and what agrees with the
religious development of mankind. We may be
perfectly certain of this, that no incarnation could
take place without an age-long previous growth

in which the providence of God prepared the way for the great event towards which the ages moved.

III

These, then, are some difficulties presented by the Incarnation in connection with space and with time. We feel sure they may be set aside, for they cannot be sustained. But, after all, they are only illustrations of difficulties. There will always be plenty more. And surely it must be so. Incarnation is a unique and a most stupendous fact. It is of such a character that it must of necessity present its difficulties. It will always transcend our comprehension. We gladly welcome the words of one who says, ' I cannot for the life of me see how the existence of One who is perfect God and perfect man can ever be completely brought within the compass of the human understanding.'[1] But that is no argument whatever against its truth.

On the contrary, it would not be Incarnation were it wholly comprehensible. It shares the quality of all ultimate realities, which is to explain innumerable problems while themselves remaining mysteries.

[1] Arlington, *A Schoolmaster's Apology*, p. 166.

The Self-judgment of Christ

The Self-judgment of Christ

IT is part of the faith of the Church that Christ did no sin. This is undeniably a tremendous thought, and it is good for us to consider at times the grounds upon which this belief is based.

I

We are sometimes met upon the very threshold of the subject with the objection that Jesus is recorded on one occasion to have expressly disclaimed any such thing as moral perfection : for when goodness was ascribed to Him by the rich young man, He declined it in the words, ' Why callest thou Me good ? None is good save one, even God.' [1]

But it must be remembered that this reply is relative to the circumstances, and to the particular individual to whom it was spoken. The young man called Christ good in the conventional superficial way in which great terms are often employed. This gave our Lord the suggestion on which to base His answer. The answer was that, strictly speaking, the term goodness is applicable to none but Deity. For the goodness of a man is acquired : that of God is natural. All human goodness is relative to human limitations : it matures with man's development. And even if the growth were free from sin, yet the goodness of man could never be measurable with that of the Uncreated. And the appropriate-

[1] S. Mark x. 18.

ness of this reply to the young man's challenge is obvious enough. He came to Christ with a somewhat serene consciousness of goodness already achieved, and with the question what else there was to do to win the approval of God. And Christ met him with the somewhat disconcerting reminder that the goodness of God is immeasurably beyond that realised by man. Goodness was a greater and a deeper thing than the young man understood.

The problem of Christ's character was not in the young man's mind. He had not come to inquire who Jesus was, but the degree of goodness necessary for a man's acceptance with his God. Christ did not introduce irrelative problems about Himself into the conversation, but answered, through a criticism on the young man's word, what was in the young man's thought. The form of the answer was not for the elucidation of Christ's person, but entirely for the young man's sake. It is designed to make him realise that goodness is something vastly greater and more difficult than he imagined it to be. That this exposition is correct is confirmed by the alternative form of our Lord's reply : Why askest thou Me concerning that which is good ?

Nor in any case is it possible to explain these words as Christ's confession of sinfulness, for to do this would be to make Him contradict Himself, and place Himself in opposition to the whole drift of the New Testament teaching.

Is it conceivable that the Evangelists could have understood the words as an acknowledgment of moral infirmity, and yet in the face of that acknowledgment have concurred unanimously in the declaration that Christ was perfect ?

The whole apostolic tradition reiterates the thought in various terms. ' He did no sin, neither was guile found in His mouth.' He was ' Like unto us in all things, sin alone except.' He was ' Holy, harmless, undefiled, separate from sinners.' ' If we say that we have no sin we deceive ourselves, and the truth is not in us.' But He was ' Jesus Christ the righteous.'

II

Among the main lines of evidence to show what Christ thought about His moral state, what was the self-judgment of Christ, may be selected three.

1. Consider what Christ said about His Death. In the upper chamber in Jerusalem, on the very night before He died, He was talking to the Twelve about His death. He said that His blood was shed for others and for the forgiveness of sins. In face of a death whose horror He keenly felt He was able to say that His death would take away from the hearts of other men the burden of sins.[1] From the hearts of others. But who is to take away that burden from the heart of Christ ? He is to die to bring the hearts of all other men peace. But who is to die to bring peace to Christ Himself ? If He were conscious like the rest of moral guilt, then someone must be found to mediate for Him. A modern writer most truly says : ' Jesus could not have spoken

[1] Herrmann's *Communion with God*, p. 74.

as He then did if He had been conscious of guilt within Himself.' [1]

2. What He said about the Judgment.

He asserted that the time would come when a judgment would be passed upon every human career, a judgment which would be perfect and therefore subject to no revision, unerring, irrevocable, divine. And when we ask by whom that judgment shall be given, expecting of course the answer that the judge is God, we find that in the place of judgment Jesus sets, not the Father, but Himself. We are of course all of us perfectly familiar with this claim. But do we realise its stupendous implications ?

We are all of us compelled at times to pass judgment on the conduct of other people. But it is a function for which we know ourselves to be utterly unqualified. There is the sense of our personal unworthiness. Who are we, being what we are, to pass any judgment on another ? To pass anything like an accurate judgment on any single human being would require a penetration into the circumstances, the moral capacities, the force of the temptation, the power of the will, the antecedents of the individual concerned, which it is impossible for us to possess. And when this prospect of passing judgment is extended so as to include the entire human race, no task more hopelessly impossible could be imposed upon a mortal man. The common sense of mankind agrees with the warning to judge nothing before the time, except provisionally, until the Lord come who will judge mankind.

[1] Herrmann's *Communion with God,* p. 75.

And yet this function of being the Judge of all mankind Christ takes upon Himself, without hesitation, without misgiving. He is certain that God has entrusted this tremendous duty to Him, and that He is competent to undertake it. He is equally certain that His decision upon any human conscience possesses finality; it cannot be subject to revision because it is absolutely true.

Now what does all this imply as to the moral condition of the Judge? He too is human like the rest. What must His moral self-judgment have been Who being human put the entire human race on the one side and Himself on the other, and considered their relation to be that of a judge towards the self-condemned?

3. Thirdly, and certainly not less impressive, is the witness of Christ's Prayers.

We commonly analyse prayer in the following kinds: petitions for ourselves, intercessions for others, thanksgivings for gifts received, praise of the glories of God, and last but certainly not least, the prayer to be forgiven. All these, especially the last, find a place in the religion of all good men. The element of penitence is bound to appear when the imperfect creature approaches the uncreated perfections. And this element of penitence intensifies with moral growth. It is not the worst of men, it is the best who express their contrition in terms of distress and self-loathing which a worldly mind will sometimes take either for sheer exaggeration or else as a proof of exceptional depravity in the past. It is neither the one nor the other. It is the self-judgment of a morally awakened soul in its conscious approach towards perfect Holiness. It is like the cry of Job when God appears. ' I have heard of Thee by the hearing of the ear : but now mine eye seeth Thee. Wherefore I abhor myself, and repent in dust and ashes.' Now it has been rightly argued that if Jesus were but an exceedingly excellent but imperfect human being then we should find the element of penitence in His prayers with an intensity corresponding to His moral loftiness. We should find the sinner surpassed in His singular sensitiveness to the least deviation from inner rectitude. But as a fact, what is it that we find ? We have many prayers of Christ, and some of them are of considerable length. They contain petitions, intercessions, thanksgiving and praise. But there is throughout one most singular omission. They never contain the element of penitence, the prayer to be forgiven. Christ said indeed, When *ye* pray say Our Father which art in Heaven . . . forgive us our trespasses. But is there any hint that Christ ever offered that prayer for Himself ? He could say, Father, forgive them, for they know not what they do. But can we conceive His saying, Father, forgive *Me* ? And if not, why ? Either this invariable omission of penitence from the personal religion of Jesus is a systematic suppression of the truth, which the whole sincerity of the situation renders utterly incredible, an alternative which it is almost a shame even to hint, or else it is the product of a serene unconsciousness of any, even the slightest, discord between His inmost self and the approval of the Righteous Father in Heaven.

Christ is conscious, as other men are not, of a communion with the Father uninterrupted by the slightest trace of sin.

III

Such then was the self-judgment of Christ upon His moral state.

Now the value of such a fact as unconsciousness of sin must depend on the moral standard which the individual possesses. If the person's moral ideals are very low it would not be difficult for him to find that he had satisfied all that was required of him. It may be possible for an ignorant and immature person to have no consciousness of sin. But that is only due to the fact that they are ignorant and immature. Their moral standard allows what a higher standard would condemn.

No doubt there have been cases like that of the rich young man who, facing the Ten Commandments, could serenely say, All these have I kept from my youth. But it is difficult not to feel that he would have expressed himself very differently if confronted by Christ's interpretation of the moral ideal in the Sermon on the Mount. It is certain that he was not what he thought he was, for he failed in the test of the great renunciation to which Christ called him.

Apply this to the case of Christ.

1. What was the moral standard by which Christ judged? We know quite well what it was. It was that contained in the Sermon on the Mount. It is the most disconcerting standard that ever was. It takes our breath away. It

overwhelms us. It talks of being perfect even as our Father in Heaven is perfect. Think of it! It talks of penetrating down beneath actions to the secret intentions of the heart, and of judging the value of deeds and words by the value of the innermost self. Men have since that day found out many inventions. They have not invented a more unearthly moral ideal than the standard propounded by Christ. Is it too much to say that they never will?

2. Now few things are more impressive than the moral penetration of Christ. The least deviation from inner rectitude was detected, judged, condemned. His capacity to apply the ideal to all the separate instances which came before Him is surely nothing less than amazing. Everyone felt it. His judgment on their individual characters was true. There is no failure anywhere. He reads their motives, penetrates thought, beyond what they say to what they think, beyond what they seem to what in reality they are. He turns upon the darkness of the human conscience the merciless searchlight of dazzling purity, in which every secret thing is shown up for what it is.

Recall how He tries everything by that Divine ideal moral light and repudiates all inferior standards of human conduct, all the pretexts and subterfuges under which human selfishness takes refuge; brushes away all bad customs, conventionalism and unrealities, under whatever length of tenure they existed, and by whatever authority they could be sanctioned. When men urged that Moses allowed divorce, the answer prompt and

34

certain came : that law is a mere concession to
human sinfulness ; it was given because of the
hardness of men's hearts ; but in the moral ideal
it is not so. Bad precepts, corrupt principles,
evil maxims in the dealings of man with man,
how He shrivelled them all up by His indignation
or His sarcasm.

3. Now this is the standard by which He
judged Himself. Tried then by this standard
of the Sermon on the Mount, this austere, awful,
confounding standard of perfection, Jesus was
conscious of no defect. It is not merely negatively
that He saw in Himself no sin. What He saw
was the positive presence of the love of all that
is good. All that the Father was and loved
Jesus also loved with all the powers of His human
soul. His human mind was absorbed exclusively
in all high thoughts. His human heart loved
nothing but what was good. His human will
was wholly directed to the achievement and
promotion of what is right, the Will of the Father
in Heaven.

Now sinlessness requires an explanation.

All our experience is that there is no man
that sinneth not. The lives of men and women
mature through sin and penitence up to goodness
it may be : but goodness marked by the fact
that it has contracted sin. One conscious and deliberate yielding up to sin, and sinlessness becomes
impossible. The sins of childhood, boyhood, youth,
remain in their effects within the man. For the
matured man is the sum total of all his conscious
good and ill. Consequently, sinlessness in manhood means sinlessness in childhood, boyhood

and youth. It means a complete resistance from the first to the insidious influence of wrong. It means an experience entirely separate from that of sinners. It means a life within the world, yet never for a single moment of it.

Assuredly such a character requires accounting for. There is only one reasonable explanation. It is that the sinlessness of Jesus is the result of an entirely unique relationship between Him and God. It is that in Christ dwelt the fulness of the Godhead bodily. It means a personal presence of Deity within Mary's Child which secured Him, through all the immaturities of childhood, boyhood and youth, with undiminished and unimpeded capacity to accomplish His redeeming task.[1]

[1] Mackintosh, *Person of Jesus Christ*, p. 414.

Christ's Revelation of God

Christ's Revelation of God

' To give the light of the knowledge of the glory of God in the face of Jesus Christ.' 2 COR. iv. 6.

THERE have been times in all our lives when we desired to know more accurately what God is; when we understood what prompted Moses to say, ' I beseech Thee, show me Thy glory.' That desire is divinely implanted. And there must be on the part of God a corresponding desire to satisfy that desire which He has created. God must long to reveal Himself to His creatures. Now, the question is, how He reveals Himself. We answer that if ever God revealed Himself to man He revealed Himself in the face of Jesus Christ. Either He has never revealed Himself at all, or Jesus Christ is His revelation; for the simple reason that Christ is the most God-like being that has ever appeared. We may derive ideas of God from other sources; and those thoughts may be considerable. But we are certain of this: that the highest and best revelation of God which we possess is that which we derive from Christ.

And if it be asked what that revelation is, we answer that it may be summed up in two words: the one is Fatherhood and the other is Love. These two comprise the sum-total of Christ's revelation concerning Him. We will confine our attention exclusively to the second of these two great terms.

We ask, then, in what way is God revealed to us in Christ.

39

RECONCILIATION

I

In the first place, God is revealed to us through Christ's teaching.

And if we ask what that teaching is, we shall almost certainly reply that the first impression which Christ's teaching about God makes upon us, is that God cares for every detail of our human life. The flowers of the field and the birds of the air were to the mind of Christ so many illustrations of providential consideration and sympathy. 'Your heavenly Father knoweth that ye have need of all these things.' There is no room for over-anxiousness. The loving-kindness, the tender compassion of God is painted for all time in the constraining picture of the father of the prodigal son. That is the first idea which we derive from the teaching of Christ on God: His boundless sympathy. This is what everybody finds in Christ's teaching.

But do we realise with equal clearness that there is another side to Christ's idea of God? The God whom Christ reveals is not all tenderness. Quite the contrary. He is a King who can order His enemies to be slain before Him. He permits the existence of a region where there is a great gulf fixed, so that they who would pass from thence cannot; where their worm dieth not, and the fire is not quenched. He warns with utmost solemnity that there is a Being who ought to be most gravely feared; One who is able to destroy both soul and body in hell.

Now, this awe-inspiring aspect of God's nature is all the more impressive because it stands in bold relief on the background of God's tenderness. And both these aspects of Christ's teaching must be carefully borne in mind. For a God who is tenderness without severity is not the same God as the Being who is both ; neither is He the God and Father of our Lord Jesus Christ.

II

But the Christian revelation of God is not only given to us through Christ's teaching, it is given to us secondly through Christ's character.

One distinctive feature of the Christian revelation is in the fact that it is not merely given through what Christ says, but also and chiefly through what Christ is.

What, then, is the character of Christ ? Without any doubt we shall reply that what impresses us first in the character of Christ is His sympathy, His inexhaustible compassion. There is a quickness of insight into every human need, and a tender selfless pitifulness for every sorrow and every pain. It is profoundly true of Him that ' in all their affliction he was afflicted ' ; ' He bore their grief and carried their sorrows.'

And all this is a revelation of the love of God.

But it is as clear as anything can be that the character of Christ presents another side. Children are sometimes taught to sing of ' Gentle Jesus, meek and mild ' : and that representation is true as far as it goes. But certainly it is not all the truth. For that gentle Jesus was capable of becoming a positive torrent of moral indignation. It is the quiet, gentle people who become a perfect

41

terror when they are really roused. And Jesus could be roused, roused even to a white, withering heat of holy wrath. There is in His character a strong but strangely curbed intensity of resentment and resistance against evil, more especially the evil of unreality. Sometimes that resentment burst forth with a force simply terrific. Think how He swept the Temple courts. Why was it that everybody retreated in helplessness before Him as He overthrew the tables of the money-changers and the seats of them that sold doves ? Was it not because they quailed before the moral indignation which bade them ' take these things hence,' silenced by the unanswerable justice of His reproach ? Above all, remember His denunciations, remember how He said, ' Woe unto you, scribes and Pharisees, hypocrites ! . . . Ye blind guides, which strain at a gnat and swallow a camel. . . . Ye are like unto whitened sepulchres, which indeed appear beautiful outward, but are within full of dead men's bones, and of all unclean-ness. Even so ye also outwardly appear righteous unto men, but within ye are full of hypocrisy and iniquity. . . . Ye serpents, ye generation of vipers, how can ye escape the damnation of hell ? ' [1]

These words are tremendous even to read. A fiery stream issued and came forth before Him. What must they have been to hear ; and to hear from the lips of that Holy One ; and to be the object against whom those withering sentences were directed ! And remember that the persons whom Christ denounced were no scandalous examples of outrageous evil-doers ; they were

[1] S. Matt. xxiii. 23–33.

42

the respectable religious circle of the day. Could anyone who heard those words ever forget them ? Would he not be haunted by them as long as he lived ? Is it not a reminiscence of them which is the background of the scene in the Revelation of S. John, when ' the kings of the earth, and the great men, and the rich men, and the chief captains, and the mighty men, and every bondman, and every free man, hid themselves in the dens and in the rocks of the mountains, and said to the mountains and rocks, Fall on us, and hide us from the face of Him that sitteth on the throne, and from the wrath of the Lamb : for the great day of His wrath is come, and who shall be able to stand ? ' [1]

What is all this but a scene clothed in imagery derived from the recollection of the wrath of the Lamb, the moral indignation of Christ ?

' He did not answer His enemies,' says a critic ; ' He annihilated them.' A writer says that Christ's character reminds him of the sun. If with its balmy light it warms the earth, it is in itself a raging furnace of consuming fire. The moral indignation of Christ withers and destroys all unworthiness.

And, in all this, the character of Christ is the revelation of the character of God. We have no right to take the gentleness of God without the severity, nor to efface the one by the help of the other, nor to imagine that the compassion reveals God any more than the indignation. God is revealed to us in both. And both of these qualities must be alike taken into account, if we want really to know what God is.

[1] Rev. vi. 15–17.

III

Thirdly, God is revealed to us through Christ's experience.

Now that experience is Incarnation. He came down to earth from heaven. And at once we say, that is the measure of God's love for us. Certainly we say true; and yet not all the truth. For if our Lord became incarnate out of love for man, it was far more out of love for His Father than out of love for us. It was love for the Father's holiness and the Father's glory which prompted the Incarnation of God's Son. It was to repair, out of love for the Father, the moral disaster wrought by man. It was anything rather than mere benevolence: it was love of holiness.

Moreover, Incarnation leads on to the Passion. Here again we say that the Passion of Christ reveals God's marvellous love. And so indeed it does. But here, again, the love that it reveals burns with a moral intensity. As we see God let His Son, His only Son, go down into the Garden of Gethsemane, and hear Him say, 'My soul is exceeding sorrowful, even unto death'; and, further, when we see Him on the Cross, and listen to that heartrending cry, 'My God, why hast Thou forsaken Me?' this is no revelation of mere compassion. The God who allowed His Son to endure all this must be a terrible God. The very last thing in the world we should think of calling Him, after this, is an easy-going Deity.

The conclusion, then, is this: God is revealed to us in Christ in three ways: Christ's teaching, Christ's character, and Christ's experience. All three converge to re-enforce the same idea. They prove that God is love.

But the question is: Who is it that God loves? And the answer is, first and above all else, He loves His eternal Son. And what is the character of that Son? He is the realisation of all goodness and truth. He is the perfection of holiness, of all that is morally beautiful and sublime. And what is the object of God's love? The love of God is primarily a love of all that is pure and lovely and of good report. It is the love of holiness. And this love of holiness is of such intensity as we cannot even conceive. For it is the love of which the Uncreated alone is capable. God loves goodness with all the strength of His will, and all the force of His being. Moreover, this love of holiness involves a corresponding detestation of what is base and bad. His detestation of evil equals in intensity His love of good. If He did not hate evil, He would not love good.

The revelation of God in Christ is of an awe-inspiring Deity, very loving, but very strong; boundless in compassion, yet unrelenting in the severity of His judgment on wrong; unsparing in self-sacrifice, yet also exacting in His moral demands upon His creatures; forgiving, indeed, but at the most tremendous cost; yearning to be reconciled with His creatures, yet inexorable.

IV

It is scarcely necessary to say that this is not the idea of God which prevails in modern life.

The popular idea of God is that He is very

good-natured and easy-going. He may be distressed and concerned by outrageous heartlessness and abominable crimes, but He is quite incapable of moral indignation. We are informed that we are to dismiss the idea of God's wrath as a great mistake, largely due to the Apostles, who mistook Christ's grief for indignation. God is represented elsewhere as so good and lenient that He overlooks everything which we want Him to overlook. Of course He forgives, without an effort, at our request. That is exactly what He is for.

Between this popular idea of God, and that of Christ, we have to make our choice. For, do not let us delude ourselves into the impression that they are the same. They are exact contradictions. And it is imperative that this should be stated with the utmost plainness. If only men would speak straight out and say: that is what Christ thought of God, but we do not agree with Him; at any rate we should know exactly where we are. But, of all fatal delusions, nothing can be worse than to accept the popular view, and imagine that it is the same thing as the revelation in Christ.

And the seriousness of the popular view is that God is brought down to the average level of commonplace men and women: with the consequence that our whole religion is changed. For our whole religion depends on our idea of God. What we think of God determines what we think of sin, and what we think of the means by which sin can be removed, and God and man become reconciled.

In Christ's revelation of God there is unutterable

46

moral glory and invigorating power. It humbles and abases us to the dust by its austere sublimity. But it is inspiring too. It is an ideal which no human imagination can transcend. It is calculated to uplift men by the very splendour of its identity with righteousness.

Above all things, it is Christ's. And the Christian axiom is that Christ knew God as men do not. This revelation of God has Christ's authority. What authority does the popular view possess ? From what source is it derived ? To ask the question is to answer it. The popular view is the insight of ordinary men. It is the product of religion diluted by worldliness. It depends on the variable spirituality of the age. It is the conception of the natural man. It is no revelation at all. It possesses no authority.

Compared with it is the authority of Christ, the perfect revelation of God. Who, as he contemplates it, can fail to hear the warning words : 'We speak that we do know, and testify that we have seen' ? Alas for us, if still He has to add : 'and ye receive not our witness'!

Christ's Teaching about His Death

between death and sin. Now Jesus was conscious
that He had no sin. Consequently He was
conscious that He was exempt from any personal
necessity to die. The Transfiguration, the radiant
glory, the open Heaven, the converse with
beings in the other world, all signified to a Jew
the right of ascension into Heaven without the
experience of death. That Christ held this
doctrine is expressly told us in S. John: 'No
man taketh My life from Me.' His relation to
death is absolutely unique. But what He can
claim for Himself as sinless, He will not accept
for His brethren's sake.

Down below on the levels of the plain lies
the human race. He will not separate Himself
from them. He will share their experience. He
talks of His decease which He must shortly
accomplish in Jerusalem. And this willing acceptance of death for others' sakes rather than
of life for His own is rewarded by the sanction
and approval of Heaven: 'This is My Beloved
Son : hear ye Him.' [1]

'Hear ye Him ' : that is to say, correct your
ideals by His and not His by yours. Rise to His
levels of sacrifice, but do not attempt to bring
His down to your own.

Then afterwards He reinforced His teaching
on the necessity of His death with impressive
urgency. 'Let these sayings sink into your ears,
for the Son of Man shall be delivered up into the
hands of men.' [2]

To their minds the whole idea is still repulsive
and utterly incredible. But Christ's rebuke of

[1] S. Mark ix. 7.　　　[2] S. Luke ix. 44.

S. Peter had taught them at least that it was not their place to correct Him. They were reduced to silence but not convinced. And they were positively afraid to ask Him anything about it.[1]

III

The third occasion when Christ foretold His death was as He approached Jerusalem.

As a rule the Master and the Apostles walked together.[2] This time He went before them, silently and alone. Evidently there was something quite unusual in His demeanour. For they were amazed. He was distant and absorbed. Some heavy burden lay upon His mind. 'And they that followed were afraid.'

Then suddenly He turned round, 'took again the Twelve,' and told them what was going to happen to Him in Jerusalem. Passion, Death, Resurrection : all these three, one after another, in vivid clearness, He set before His bewildered followers. They could not possibly misunderstand His words.[3] But they still saw no use in such a destiny. They could not see how He could save His nation by His death. They lived in a world of totally different ideas.

IV

Our Lord then on these three great occasions, at Cæsarea Philippi, at the Transfiguration, and

[1] S. Luke ix. 45.   [2] S. Mark x. 32–34.
[3] S. Luke xviii. 34.

at the final ascent to Jerusalem, insisted with emphasis and in detail on the fact and the necessity of His death. But so far He had insisted upon the fact rather than upon the meaning. He now proceeded to give suggestions about what it meant. This He did chiefly in two words. He described His death as a Ransom and as a Covenant.

1. He said that 'the Son of Man came not to be ministered unto but to minister, and to give His life a ransom for many.'[1] Now here, if we are to understand aright, we must put ourselves back into the time of Christ, and attempt to realise what ideas the term ransom would convey to those who heard it. In Jewish circles what a ransom meant was the price paid down to emancipate a slave or release from captivity a prisoner of war.

The Psalmist says that wealthy men cannot deliver their relatives from death by the payment of a ransom. The prayer of the Maccabean patriot Eleazar was : ' Make my blood an expiatory offering for Israel, and take my life as their ransom.' And the Jewish historian praises the heroes of the Wars of Independence because they became as it were a ransom, or expiation, for the sins of the people.[2]

These illustrations explain what our Lord's expression, ' to give His life a ransom for many,' would convey to His contemporaries, namely that His death would secure their deliverance from sin.

2. Then again He called His death a Covenant.

[1] S. Mark x. 45.
[2] Murray, *D. B.*, s.v. ' Jesus Christ,' p. 412.

It was in the upper chamber in the Holy City at the institution of the Eucharist. He said: 'This is My Blood of the Covenant which is shed for many.' [1]

Now to us of the twentieth century this language sounds obsolete and strange. That is the difficulty. It does not convey to the modern mind any profound religious conception. It belongs to a circle of religious ideas which have passed completely out of use. The question therefore is what it meant for those to whom Christ said it.

He said it on the very night before He died and while He inaugurated the great memorial of the Passion. He spoke of covenant, and blood and shedding, and added that its effect would be extensive, and expressly for the forgiveness of sins.

Now what would all this suggest to any Jew ? The language would, beyond any doubt, awaken a whole train of thought, and carry their minds back to the covenant by sacrifice at Sinai between God and Israel, when Moses said of the sacrifice, this is the blood of the Covenant.

They would certainly understand that just as the ancient sacrifice had united God with Israel, so the death of Christ would effect a union between God and the Kingdom of Christ. And when He said, ' Do this in remembrance of Me,' they would understand that He was instituting the Eucharist as a permanent memorial of His death, and therefore concentrating their devotion upon His self-offering.

[1] S. Mark xiv. 24.

V

Finally there is the teaching about His death to be gathered from Gethsemane.

1. We surely must agree with those who say that the Agony in the Garden cannot be accounted for by any mere natural shrinking from pain and death. It is a psychological fact that great elevation of spirit has not only rendered human beings almost insensible to physical pain, but filled them with a joyous confidence, sustaining them to the very end. The example of S. Stephen is one of sacrifice made with indomitable courage and even gladness. And his is only the first name in a long succession. Nor is it possible to account for the difference between the martyrs and Christ by difference of temperament. For it is their reliance upon Christ which made them strong. Why then did they face death serenely while He their Lord and their supporter was crushed in the anguish of indescribable distress ?

2. The only real accounting for it is that death meant for Him what it could not mean for them.

We must see it in the circle of Jewish ideas. Remember that this is part of a sinless experience. All through His human career, contact with human unworthiness had filled Him with deep pain. It was sin which extorted from Him the reproval : 'O faithless and perverse generation, how long shall I be with you, how long shall I suffer you ? ' It was this which made Him exclaim : 'O righteous Father, the world hath not known Thee.' But what sustained Him all through His contact with

the evil of the world was His uninterrupted communion with the Father in Heaven. But now,
as He draws near to the last experience, He knows
that death for Him will mean so close, so intimate
a self-identity with sin that His very communion
with the Father will be overclouded and even
darkened. It is that isolation which He fears,
and hence an anguish which is to us almost
inconceivable.

Therefore because He was so pure He recoiled
in horror from this burden of human sins. If
only it were possible, let mankind be saved some
other way. Death for Christ must mean to
experience the sinner's isolation from the Father,
acutely aware of all that this isolation means.
Therefore He pleaded with such concentration
and intensity that He might be spared if it were
consistent with the Holy Will. Torn between
the conflicting entreaties, ' Father, save Me from
this hour,' and ' Father, glorify Thy Name,' He
endures the bitterest anguish of which mortal
nature can be capable.

But even while He prayed the light had
come. His human mind saw plainly that His
death was the Father's Will. Henceforth He
could not wish to be delivered. He issues forth
in wonderful dignity and self-possession.[1] He
cannot ask for the legions of angels which would
be at His service for the asking. For ' how then
should the Scriptures be fulfilled that thus it must
be ? ' He sees that His death will realise the
eternal counsel of the Father. By it the Scriptures
will be fulfilled. The providential guidance of

[1] S. Matt. xxvi. 54.

the world has been leading up to this, and in His death will achieve a marvellous consummation.

VI

We have grouped these scenes together.

What they show is this : How large a place His death occupied in the words of Christ. And if in His words still more within His thoughts.

This then is the explanation which Christ has given us of His death.

As we look back on it there probably comes a sense of disappointment. It is obviously fragmentary and incomplete. There are hints and suggestions ; but there is no systematic view. There is a striking difference between these utterances and the doctrine of Reconciliation in S. Paul. And it may be true that we should not see our way if left entirely to ourselves to have constructed the one out of the other. It may be so.

But if this meagreness disappoints we surely ought to realise that such comparative meagreness is exactly what we ought to expect.

There are obvious reasons on the side of the Disciples and also on the side of Christ.

1. On the side of the Disciples.

Remember that the thought of Jesus' death was peculiarly repugnant and intolerable to His disciples' minds. It ran entirely counter to their Jewish presuppositions. It seemed to them to mean no less than frustration of all their hopes. It meant ruin and failure.

But even worse than that. The idea of crucifixion filled them with especial horror, because

to their Jewish way of thinking such a form of
death implied the curse of God. We can scarcely
realise the loathing and abhorrence, the shrinking
as from despair and judgment, which the disciples
must have felt when Christ said He would be
crucified. No doubt He added the promise that
He would rise again. But the promise did not
for them relieve the horror of the idea. They
could not help exclaiming, "That be far from
Thee, Lord. This shall not be unto Thee." Well,
He might rebuke them if He pleased. Rebuke them
He did. But He only reduced them to silence.
He did not in the least convince. They were
impervious at the time to anything approaching
conviction. They simply refused to believe. How
then could He teach them of Redemptive Sacrifice,
of Justification through His Blood ?

2. Then again there are reasons on the side
of Christ.

If Christ was the Redeemer of the world, that
is the very reason of all others why we ought
not to expect a doctrine of Redemption from
Him. If He were a mere instructor in religious
principles, a lecturer in theology, or a systematic
theologian, then certainly He would naturally
expatiate on the principles by which mankind
might be redeemed. The less He had to do
with working it out the more disposed He might
be to discuss the subject. But if He is Himself
the Redeemer, the Person by Whom the world
would be redeemed, then His mission was not
to talk about it but to do it.

To expect the Redeemer to pause in the middle
of the redemptive process, in order to give a

systematic account of the theory of Redemption, is one of the most unnatural and unreasonable of all possible expectations. If that were what the Gospel narrative contained, all the critics in the world would be unanimous in pronouncing it no better than fiction.

It is profoundly true that Christ did not come so much to preach the Gospel as so to live that there might be a Gospel to preach.

The Apostolic Interpretation of Christ

The Apostolic Interpretation of Christ [1]

'Ye shall be My witnesses.' ACTS i. 8.

THE Apostolic interpretation of Christ is chiefly concerned with three things : His Kingdom, His Person, and His Death. His Death was a propitiation, His Kingdom was world-wide, His Person was Divine.

We are, however, confronted to-day with an extreme school of critics which is prepared to set all this aside. They tell us that, while this is undoubtedly what the Apostles affirm, Jesus Himself has nowhere said as much, nor anything like it. They tell us that the estimate which Jesus formed of His Death, His Person, and His Kingdom, was far more modest than that which the Apostles maintain.

They say that if the Apostles interpret Christ's death as the reconciliation between God and man, this was merely because they found the expression ready to hand, and borrowed the notion from the Jews ; but that the Apostles thereby introduced into the new religion a theory of Redemption completely different from that which Jesus Himself believed.

They say, moreover, that the Apostolic interpretation of Christ's person is equally misleading : that the notion of His essential equality with the

[1] Preached in S. Paul's Cathedral on the First Sunday after Easter, 1915.

Father is entirely wrong, being nothing more than an unfortunate speculation borrowed from the metaphysical Greek.

They tell us, lastly, that the Apostolic conception of the world-wide Church, or Kingdom of Christ, goes far beyond the Master's mind, for He only thought of the house of Israel, while this other idea is borrowed from the world-wide Empire of Rome.

These critical opinions on Christ's Kingdom and Person and Death are supported by enormous learning and acuteness. They are no longer confined to foreign languages, or to ponderous monographs only accessible to the studious few. They are popularised in eminently readable and attractive forms. They circulate everywhere. And it has long become imperatively necessary for Churchmen to consider the value of such criticisms upon the Church's Faith.

I

In the first place, then, let us consider the Apostolic interpreters.

For the first reflection which these critical theories provoke is surely this : You tell us that the Apostles, in their interpretation of Christ, borrowed one idea from the Jews, and that this was mistaken ; and another idea from the Greeks, and that this was misleading ; and another idea from the Romans, and that this misrepresented Him. They interpreted Christ from three distinct nationalities, and each interpretation was wrong. Whether they contemplated His person, His work, or His kingdom (three matters surely fundamental), they misunderstood them all. According to you, the Apostles had a perfect genius for misinterpretation. They were obliged to interpret Christ either in Latin, or Hebrew, or Greek, simply because no other languages were within their reach. If they failed conspicuously, not in details merely, but in essential principles, in the very foundations on which the new religion was built, failed altogether on every one of these momentous themes, it is, to say the least, somewhat singular.

For these Apostolic interpreters of Christ had certain undeniable advantages. They had the advantage of a nearness to the historic Jesus which we moderns cannot share. They were the recipients of His direct and immediate influence. Now, it is proverbial that a great personality is known, not only by what he says and what he does, but by the way he stamps his genius upon his contemporaries, and, indeed, upon the succeeding generations. If the Apostles had not believed that Jesus redeemed us, and that He rose from the dead, it is highly probable that we should never have heard His name. Indeed, if He were no more than some of His critics think, there hardly appears sufficient reason why we should. We have come to know Him because of His Apostles' belief. But then their belief about Him requires accounting for. What is the meaning of a personality which provokes so extraordinary an explanation? Is it a usual thing to interpret religious genius in terms of metaphysical equality with God? or to describe a human death as the only means of reconciling earth and heaven ? Has this ever been seriously attempted elsewhere, either before or since ? Does not the uniqueness of the Apostles' estimate suggest uniqueness in that which created it ? Is it reasonable to dismiss the Faith of Christendom as misunderstanding and exaggerated admiration ? If the Apostles borrowed these great conceptions from the Hebrew and the Latin and the Greek, was it not because the sublimity of Christ made it impossible to account for Him by anything less ?

Conversely, if the Apostolic interpretation of Christ was fundamentally wrong, surely men ought to be exceedingly cautious before they accept any other. If the first century, under the immediate direction of the historic Jesus, put entirely false constructions upon His person and His death, what security can we have that the twentieth century will not do the same ? Doubtless the modern mind has developed a critical power to which the primitive mind was a stranger ; but the valuation of religious person-ality depends neither on critical acuteness nor on learning, it depends on religious insight and spiritual capacity. Whatever our superiority in other respects, are we better qualified in this respect than they ? If the Apostles interpreted Christ in a certain manner because they approached Him with certain ideas, do not modern critics precisely the same ? Doubtless the presup-positions of the critic are very different from those of S. John or S. Paul, but are they necessarily one bit more true ? And if the Latin and the Hebrew and the Greek failed to interpret Jesus aright, is there not the same liability for the German and the English and the French ?

Look at the history of the modern interpretations of Christ. The nineteenth century was occupied throughout with attempts to reconstruct the Son of Man from a modern critical point of view. Their acuteness was wonderful, their patience untiring, their learning immense. Their criticism has taught us in many ways to understand the Apostolic age as it was never understood before. But what is the value considered as an interpretation of Christ ? One after another remarkable works have been composed. One after another they have been cast aside. An able critic, who has read some hundred of these works and written their history, comes to the conclusion that ' such a Jesus as is painted by this research . . . never existed. His figure is a fanciful picture, sketched by rationalism, revivified by liberalism, wrongfully represented by modern theology as the result of historical science.' [1]

Now, the truthfulness of this verdict is becoming increasingly recognised far and wide. It is attested by the rapidity with which each successive interpretation disappears. This is their invariable fate. They fail to satisfy. It is one thing to set the Apostolic interpretation aside. It is quite a different matter to set another in its place ; another which shall secure anything more than an ephemeral popularity ; a reconstruction which shall last and live, which shall have power to

[1] Schweitzer, *The Quest of the Historic Jesus.* Cf. Loofs, *What is the Truth about Jesus Christ ?* p. 43.

convert and recreate. Surely, the moral of all this is plain. If the Apostolic interpreters were fundamentally mistaken, then to ascertain with any certainty who Jesus is, becomes a positively hopeless undertaking.

II

Secondly, consider why it is that so many modern critics reject the Apostolic interpretation of Christ.

It is caused by the modern idea of history. History is studied to-day as a phenomenon strictly within the limits of the purely natural. History shows what men have thought and what men have done. It records their opinions and beliefs. It contains so much natural fact and so much psychology. But it deliberately rules out the supernatural world altogether. In the school of modern history, which is entitled scientific, the question whether such a Being as God exists is simply set aside. That question does not come within its province.

Now, of course, this view of history, the scientific view, is not only perfectly legitimate; it is, for its purpose, of quite peculiar worth. Just as a chemist can analyse the stuffs of which the earth is made, without asking the question whether they had a Maker; just as the astronomer can form a map of the stars, without inquiring whether the heavens declare the glory of God or only the cleverness of Isaac Newton, and can even go so far as to say that, for his particular purpose, he has no need of the hypothesis of a

Deity; so the scientific historian can tabulate religions and compare them together as so many opinions and beliefs of the being called man, without investigating the spiritual problem whether there is a higher order of being called God. This restriction of study into departments has its obvious uses, because our capacities are so limited, and we often understand things better when we concern ourselves with only one department of the universe at a time. But it needs to be most carefully remembered that a limited department of the universe can only yield a limited account of the meaning of the universe as a whole.

Now, where the trouble rises is when the scientific historian confronts Jesus Christ. For Jesus is a figure in history. With Jesus, therefore, the historian must deal. But the historian, having started on the principle that history is confined to the purely natural, has already ruled the supernatural out. Consequently he is driven to do one of two things: either he must force Jesus Christ into the limits of the strictly human, rejecting every thought of His Divinity, and of His being the Reconciler of God and mankind; or else he must confess that history, being within the limits of the purely natural, is incompetent to explain Him, and that Christ belongs to the sphere of religion and of faith. The majority of modern critics unhappily refuse to recognise the artificial character of the restrictions under which, as scientific historians, they labour. They have isolated one part of human nature from the rest, and then insist in regarding that part as if it were the whole. There are, however, critics who confess that Jesus Christ cannot be accounted for within the limits of the merely human and the earthly.

And most assuredly it is these latter who are right. For the life of man within the realm of nature is radically incomplete. Of course, the religions of the world can be studied as so much human belief. But sooner or later the question must be faced, Does this belief correspond with reality or does it not ? The scientific historian can record that a certain Man adopted a devotional attitude and uttered some devotional expressions in Gethsemane ; that He appeared profoundly agitated, but presently emerged in peace. But it is impossible for the same historian, considered as a man, and therefore capable of religion, not to inquire, Was that utterance in the Garden simply a human cry into an unheeding Universe, or is there a corresponding Personal Reality who heard ? Is there such a Being as Deity, or is there not ? And if there is, then is this world a stage with God for the audience ? Does He merely watch the play, look on, approving what is well enacted, condemning what is badly done ? Is He only a passive spectator, while the age-long drama of humanity unfolds before Him ? Or is He actively engaged in advancing and maturing the same ? Is there such a thing as a providential government of the world ? Is God in history ?

Now, the religious mind is compelled to answer, Yes, He is. For a God Who is not in history is not really God at all. Either there is no God, or else God is in the life of man. The religious

72

development of man is not the unaided product of man's activity. Humanity is under superhuman influence and control. There is an aim and a purpose running throughout it. God has been working in history to His own great ends. Our life is a confluence of the forces of two worlds, the human and the Divine. Faith cannot be confined within the sphere of nature. It will break out beyond its earthly horizon. It persists in claiming that there are powers in human life derived from a realm which is beyond the scientific historian's reach; and that there is much in life which nothing but the supernatural can explain.

Descending, then, from these generalities to particulars, the Christian view of history affirms that human life was slowly matured in such a way as to admit the Incarnation. There was that outstanding marvel, the religious growth of Israel. It was divinely guided. The great religious products of the chosen race, its ethical monotheism, its lofty conception of God's awful righteousness, its corresponding sense of sin, its ever-deepening ideas of sacrifice and propitiation : these were consequences of the providential pressure of revelation upon the Jewish mind; they are substantially and essentially true.

When, therefore, the time arrived for the interpretation of Christ, His interpreters explained His death in terms of Godward offering, and His person in terms of equality with the Father, and His kingdom in terms of the Universal Church, not merely because these terms lay ready to their hands, nor because their minds were naturally filled with these ideas ; but because it was providentially determined that it should be so. The deeply spiritual religion of the Jews, the majestic, world-wide dominion of Rome, the wondrous metaphysical depth of the intellectual Greek, that finest of all instruments of human thought and speech : all these were providentially furnished to interpret to the mind of man the mysteries of God made flesh. These Apostolic interpretations were not unfortunate mistakes which might have been avoided had the Apostles been superseded by certain clever critics of to-day. They were part of ' the determinate counsel and foreknowledge of God.' They happened when ' the fulness of the time was come.' Christ's interpreters from Jerusalem have no need to abdicate in favour of the interpreters from Berlin.

If we believe in the Incarnation, is it possible to say less than this ? And surely, if God is anywhere in history at all, then certainly God was in Christ. And then, it is not a thing conceivable that the Incarnation should be true, and yet the true character of Christ's person, kingdom, and death should be hopelessly distorted by His own Apostles. Make what allowances you will for human infirmity and misunderstanding, it is impossible to believe that Christ can be the great Revelation of God to man, and yet that the fundamental characteristics of that Revelation should have been misrepresented to the world during the first two thousand years of its existence entirely through the fact of Apostolic incompetence.

III

Finally, there is a most significant fact which cannot be omitted. Christ left Himself to the Apostolic interpretation.

It is a most extraordinary thing, familiar as we are with it. He thoroughly understood their narrow limits. This appears all through the Gospel on almost every page. He rebukes their prosaic unintelligence. He sighs over their blindness in the realm of the spirit. He is thwarted by their reluctance to accept His intuitions.

And yet He wrote down nothing ; not a single word. Everything we know about Him has reached us through the medium of their minds. He combined a penetrating consciousness of their limitations with a perfectly serene assurance of their capacity. He said, ' Ye shall be My witnesses.' Do we realise the thrilling sublimity of His confidence that they will not fundamentally misinterpret Him or caricature Him after He has gone ? What is the secret of His confidence ? It is this : ' When the Spirit of Truth is come, He will guide you.' That is the reason why ' ye shall be My witnesses.' Christ's view of history did not leave God out. He entrusted those men with the biggest task ever imposed on mortals : that of interpreting His person and His work to the human race. Christ trusted the Apostles, and He trusted the Church, of which they were the presidents. Christ trusted them. I would therefore say deliberately : I am prepared to do the same.

The Problem of Reconciliation before Saul the Rabbi

The Problem of Reconciliation before Saul the Rabbi

'Who shall deliver me?' Rom. vii. 24.

SAUL of Tarsus, in the days before his conversion to Christianity, was a deeply religious man. He could not merely acquiesce in the religion of his country in the way in which a man can acquiesce in the fashions with regard to a suit of clothes. He appropriated it because he believed it, and believing it he preached it for all that he was worth. In point of fact religion was his ruling passion. His deepest desire was to be reconciled with his Maker. That was the aim on which his heart was set. He wanted to be in union with his God. And since it was impossible for a man of his extraordinary energy to do anything by halves, he threw himself into this desire with all his force. He concentrated upon this one main purpose the various powers of his richly gifted nature.

He worked, he prayed, he struggled, he repented, he read the Scriptures, he put himself under the guidance of one of the noblest Pharisees of his time. He followed out the rules of his religion. He persevered in them. He surpassed most of his contemporaries. He was known in the devout circles at Jerusalem as an exceedingly religious and spiritually minded young man.

And yet in spite of all these efforts he could

not secure the one thing on which his heart was set. He could not believe that God was reconciled. He could not bring himself to think that any efforts of his were sufficient to secure so glorious a result.

I

Saul the Rabbi has been severely taken to task for this by a clever modern writer of the Jewish nation.[1] According to his opinion, Saul's view of reconciliation is so much unnecessary fuss. It may have been natural to so strange a character, but in reality it is much ado about nothing.

God, as understood in the Jew's religion, is certainly great and awful, but He is also kindly and pitiful. His relations with Israel are similar to those of a human father to his children. Of course He grieves over His children's faults. He rewards and He punishes, He chastises and He forgives. He loves His children. He wants them to be happy and good.

And He has provided a means by which their happiness and their goodness may be secured. That means is the Law. The Law is His gracious gift to Israel. The Law is partly moral, partly ceremonial. There are a great number of commands.[2] But apparently the more the better, because the more commandments God has given the more opportunities of honouring Him by obedience, and the more means for self-purification and self-control.

[1] C. Montefiore, *Judaism and S. Paul*, p. 27.
[2] *Ibid.* p. 29.

The observance of these laws is no burden.[1] On the contrary, how could it be ? They are given by a God Who is perfectly wise and perfectly good; Who therefore knows what is best for you. He has given them because in their observance you will find satisfaction and joy, the highest life on earth, and the most blissful life hereafter.[2] Consequently the possession of the Law of God was their glory and their joy.

Well, but what if the Law were not observed ? What if it were broken ? It is undoubtedly true that the Jews do not all observe the Law, ' on the contrary all more or less fail to fulfil its injunctions.'[3] Well, what then ? Of course God is angry. He is very angry, especially with hardened sinners who violate the Law in open mockery and revolt. But every Jew has broken the Law more or less. Does not God's anger therefore rest on every one of them ? It seems a bad business. The Law is no joy now. Instead of a privilege it is a burden. Instead of a joy it is sorrow and gloom. What then is to be done ?

Judaism, we are informed, is ' equal to the occasion.'[4] Of course God is angry. But then He knows whereof we are made. The Law was meant for man and not for angels. ' It was given to beings who by their very constitution and history were bound to make frequent lapses and to fall often into sin.' ' The Rabbinic Jew did not worry himself much about the theory that the whole Law (with all its enactments) has to

[1] C. Montefiore, *Judaism and S. Paul*, p. 31.
[2] *Ibid.* p. 32.　[3] *Ibid.* p. 38.　[4] *Ibid.* p. 40.

be obeyed. He took a practical view of the situation.' God was kind and merciful and compassionate, not merely awful and holy and severe.

'And the difficulty of the Law must not be exaggerated.'[1] The average man often fulfils many divine behests, although no doubt there is not a command which he could not fulfil more perfectly than is actually the case. Still, partial failures lead to improvement and advance.

And then repentance makes everything quite right.[2] Let a man repent but a very little and God will forgive very much. On the Day of Atonement man and God are engaged in doing nothing else than repentance and forgiveness.[3] This gives the Jew a fresh start, a clean slate.

Thus 'for every decent Israelite there is a place in the life to come.'[4] And the average man, as well as the saint, is able to feel with regard to the Law that 'its ways are ways of pleasantness and all its paths are peace.'

Thus Judaism is a joyous, simple religion.[5] It is a religion of the healthy minded. It is, however, admitted that this religion of the Rabbi's does not readily produce the mystic temper which loses itself in God.[6]

---

[1] C. Montefiore, *Judaism and S. Paul*, p. 41.
[2] *Ibid.* p. 42.   [3] *Ibid.* p. 43.   [4] *Ibid.* p. 44.
[5] *Ibid.* p. 48.   [6] *Ibid.* p. 50.

II

This was in all probability the religion of the Pharisees in the time of Christ. Why was it not sufficient for Saul ? He was himself a Pharisee, and his father was a Pharisee before him. He was instructed by a Pharisee of the noblest type. Why was it that this view of reconciliation, which was quite enough for them, seemed to his eyes mean, wretched, and inadequate ? Might not the Pharisees of Jerusalem quite plausibly turn upon him with the rebuke, This religion was good enough for your fathers : it satisfies the spiritual requirements of older, more experienced men than yourself. Surely it ought to be good enough for you.

Now the reasons why it was impossible for Saul to be satisfied with this idea of reconciliation were these :

1. First, because of the powerlessness of law. The Law of God, or the moral ideal, Saul would say is ' holy and righteous and good.' [1] He accumulates epithets to express the elevation of its character. It is, he gladly acknowledges, perfectly sublime. He accords it the tribute of his admiration. Very well, it may be answered, then go and do it.

At which he would reply, That is entirely another thing. I admire the moral law in my better self, but there is unfortunately another side to the question. For look you, I am the proprietor

[1] Rom. vii. 12.

G 2

of numerous inclinations, desires and passions, clamorous, persistent, demonstrative, unruly, each one striving for the satisfaction of itself. And when the ghostly shadow of the moral law comes in, the fact is that its suggestions do not manage to secure the attention they deserve. If the moral law had might as it unquestionably has right, it would certainly rule the world. But it does not possess that might. It has no strength to get itself obeyed. Not only that; it provokes me to resist. When the law appears exclaiming, Thou shalt not: that is immediately the thing of all others that I want to do. It is not the fault of the law. The fault lies in my own perversity. We all know how true this is. There was a most successful advertisement in London some time since which printed in conspicuous letters the words Don't Look: and of course forthwith everybody gazed intently. Prohibition increases desire. I had not known sin except the Law had said, Thou shalt not covet.

And again, this is not the fault of the moral law. If there could have been a law given capable of giving life then no doubt righteousness should have been by the law. But law cannot give life. On the contrary: the practical effect of the moral ideal is to pass judgment on all who fail to fulfil it; and the higher you raise the standard the more certainly does it condemn. If the mere letter of the law condemns, still more does its spirit. Then the result of this beautiful moral ideal is simply this: it becomes to men a ministration of condemnation and a ministration of death.

2. Secondly, because of the powerlessness of his repentance.

Saul knew very well that God was merciful and that God would forgive. The difficulty was not there. The difficulty lay in the powerlessness of his repentance to rid himself of sin. Sin was not like a splash of mud upon the face which could easily be washed away. It was no mere action which left the character pretty much unchanged. But it had penetrated down into the very fibre of his being. His very self had been identified with it. He had deliberately uttered his real nature in this sinful deed. How could repentance rid his soul of that ? His character was built up of all his past. He was the sum total of all past infidelities. His very repentance was modified by his sinfulness. It was not adequate. It could not be. He was repentant, of course, sincerely. But to be repentant is one thing, to be holy is another. And how could that mere penitence unite the sinful self with the all holy God ? That was Saul's difficulty.

III

These, then, are the two contrasted ideas of reconciliation : that of the ordinary Jew and that of Saul.

1. Can we doubt for a single moment which of them is the deeper view, which of them is the more penetrating, and which the more superficial ? Is not Saul's conception of the comparative ineffectiveness of moral ideals to get themselves realised and fulfilled endorsed by the deepest

experience of mankind at its best ? Is not his view of the power of deliberate evil over the heart and the will of man profoundly true to the facts of moral life ?

Here let us remember that we are considering a man of most exceptional religious gifts. Saul of Tarsus was no worldly person converted to a pious kind of life. He was no ordinary average mortal with the usual mixture of apathy and faith. He was endowed with a spiritual penetration which has been rarely equalled. He was not a moderately religious person, but of extraordinary religious intensity. He was certainly one of the spiritual experts of mankind. His letters show that the ideas of the great prophets of Israel had taken possession of his very soul. The awful Holiness of God was no mere phrase for him. His spiritual insight enabled him to understand why his ancestors trembled in God's presence ; why they dared not draw too near to Him ; why they cried, In Thy sight shall no man living be justified.

That sense of personal worthlessness which came upon Israel's best came on Saul with overwhelming effect. He had entered into the Jew's religion at its highest. His character responded to all this. It was precisely because he was so spiritual, so penetrating, so devout, that he took in and assimilated in all their solemnity these great ideas.

2. It was precisely this sense of need which paved the way for Saul to appreciate the religion of reconciliation through Christ.

And it is precisely the absence of this sense

of need which renders many men to-day incapable of real assent to such a religion. Every man his own redeemer is a phrase which commends itself to the independence of the natural man, to his dislike to find himself under an obligation to anyone. God made me a man, I made myself a good man, said an ancestor of our own centuries ago. Then Augustine answered, If that is true you have gone one better than the Almighty. But the spirit which prompted that independence of a redeemer is as strong as ever in the British mind.

There is a strange and piteous tendency in modern religion to revert to the theory of reconciliation as held by the Pharisees in the time of Christ. A religion of redemption by Christ leaves men cold if they have no sense of personal need. It has been said, and it is profoundly true, that Christianity has in these days first to create the sense of need to which its doctrine can appeal. If men are competent to supply all their own spiritual needs and to secure their own reconciliation unaided, then Christ the Redeemer becomes a superfluity. He will be either interpreted in inferior senses, or He will be dispensed with altogether.

The religion of the Pharisees will suffice so long as a man believes in his own ability. But when misgivings increase, and the distance between himself and his Maker deepens, and the gulf appears insurmountable by any effort of his own, then he is open, but not before, to the meaning of the Christian offer.

S. Paul's Conception of the Death of Christ

S. Paul's Conception of the Death of Christ

'There is therefore now no condemnation to them that are in Christ Jesus.' ROM. viii. 1.

WE have already seen in our previous subject how Saul of Tarsus, in the days before his conversion, threw the whole energies of his richly gifted nature into the effort to be reconciled with his Maker. We have seen also that in spite of all his strenuous and persistent efforts he failed entirely to acquire that peace with God upon which his heart was set. Further, we have seen that the reasons of his failure were two. First, because he realised very deeply the powerlessness of moral ideals to get themselves obeyed; and secondly, because he realised very deeply the penetrating and paralysing power of sin, which does not pass over the surface of our nature leaving the self unchanged, but on the contrary sinks in and becomes part and parcel of our inmost personality, clouding the affections and enfeebling the will, so that our best repentance is compromised by our past, and the offering of an adequate reparation to the Divine Holiness is rendered utterly impossible.

Now it is clear that a man who has arrived at the certainty that he cannot deliver himself nor reconcile himself with his Maker is on the high road to appreciate a religion in which a redeemer is presented. If a man is convinced that he is entirely unable to redeem himself, he is naturally disposed to welcome one who can redeem him. Consequently Saul of Tarsus was so far in a receptive state towards Christianity.

Nevertheless he could not believe in the new religion. And this for what appeared to him the most conclusive reasons. For his theory about the Christ or the Messiah was that he must be a visible king enthroned at the head of God's people in Jerusalem. The one incredible thing was that the Christ could die. The conception of the suffering Christ, the dying Christ is familiar enough to the mind of any Christian, but it does not appear to have been realised in the period before the Christian era. Neither the 53rd chapter of Isaiah's prophecies nor the 22nd Psalm were in those days commonly applied to the Christ that was to be. Consequently when Saul heard that Jesus of Nazareth was dead he considered that any pretensions the prophet might have made to Christhood were thereby conclusively refuted. How was it possible that the Almighty should permit His Christ to die? Saul had no use for a dead Christ. It was a contradiction in terms. And what made things if possible still worse was the form which that death had taken. For the Jew regarded crucifixion with peculiar abhorrence. Was it not written in the Law, Cursed is every one that hangeth upon a tree? He then Who died upon that Cross could only be considered as under the malediction of God. Jesus of Nazareth had claimed to be the Christ. His death proved that this is exactly what He was not. It proved that God had rejected Him. That death was the Divine refutation of a blasphemous claim.

S. PAUL'S CONCEPTION OF CHRIST'S DEATH

Saul was accordingly convinced that Jesus of Nazareth was no better than a mere deceiver. He would have cordially endorsed the Jewish taunt, let Him deliver Him now if He will have Him. Saul of course was quite familiar with the Christian assertion that Jesus had risen from the dead. But he gave no credit whatever to the idea. It was the death which was decisive. It loomed so large in his eyes, and seemed so overwhelming, that he was quite unable to take this other, strange and badly attested, report. Naturally therefore the new religion roused his sternest opposition. It was his simple duty to stamp it out by every means in his power. And he threw himself with his accustomed energy and concentration into the attempt to crush the Christian Church.

Then came the memorable day outside Damascus. Saul saw in sudden radiance, and in all the glory of Heaven, a figure whom he does not know. He heard the Voice : Saul, Saul, why persecutest thou Me ? He answered, in his ignorant wonderment, Who art Thou ? He heard the reply, I am Jesus Whom thou persecutest. Thrown into utter confusion, he simply trembled with astonishment, confronted with the splendour of this heavenly vision which thenceforth and for ever completely revolutionised his outlook on life, his thoughts of God, and his innermost condition. Outwardly blinded, but inwardly enlightened, he began, first in the house in the city, and afterwards in the solitude of Arabia, to think out for himself the implications of that Divine Revelation granted him outside Damascus Gate.

RECONCILIATION

I

Let us try to follow out some of the principal changes in Saul's theology.

1. The first was that he gained a new idea of Jesus' position. He knows now that, after all, Jesus *is* the Christ. Jesus is the divinely chosen Head of the chosen people. He is the consummation and the glory of Israel's age-long development. And therefore Saul must abandon his former theories of what the Christ must do and be. The thing to him incredible is true. His notion of a visible Christ enthroned in Jerusalem must now be replaced by the fact of an invisible Christ enthroned in Heaven. His inferior, half-materialistic conceptions of Christ's place and work must be exchanged for a purely spiritual conception such as had never entered his thoughts before. If he had known Christ after the flesh he must now know Christ after the Spirit. This meant an extraordinary uplifting of his old ideas, necessitated by the glory of the vision which he had seen.

2. The second change in the religious outlook of Saul was that he gained a new idea of Jesus' character.

Hitherto he had maintained that Jesus of Nazareth was a mere deceiver, and therefore very low down in the moral scale. But now that interpretation must be thrown to the rubbish heap of the unworthy and the false. The sight of Jesus in the heavenly glory had expelled that misconception for ever. A new interpretation must be found in accordance with the facts. But what did that glory of Jesus mean? Remember that it was the glory of heaven, that it signified close proximity to God. Remember also with what impressive force that nearness to God would come upon a man whose deepest yearning had been after nearness to God, after reconciliation with his Maker. Remember further the great traditions of the religious Israelite. He knew how his forefathers shrank back from the presence of God; how the Sacred Temple where God dwelt was fenced in awful solitude from all intrusion of sinful men; how holy men cried out in terror when they had even seen in a vision the King, the Lord of Hosts; how the Psalmist sang, In Thy sight shall no man living be justified. How then could Jesus of Nazareth stand just there where Saul would give his life to stand, and knew too painfully well that he dared not and could not stand? Why was this Jesus the solitary exception in the glory of God? Why, indeed, unless that close proximity to the awful Holiness signified a moral perfection in the Man Jesus Himself. Yes, this was the only possible interpretation. Doubtless Saul had heard Christians say this thing before, only he absolutely refused to credit what they said. But now the fact was simply forced upon him. It must be so. Jesus could not endure to stand in the glory where Saul had seen Him unless He was untouched by the moral imperfections of sinful men.

3. There was yet a third change which came in Saul's theology. He gained a new idea of the meaning of Jesus' death.

Hitherto, remember, that death appeared in

his opinion as the Divine rejection of Jesus and
His claim. That interpretation must now have
filled Saul's heart with shame and humiliation.
For it is ever a deeply humbling experience to
have misread a message of God to the human
soul. Rejection was what the death of Jesus
could not be. The question to be answered is,
What was it ? Well, clearly it was the death of
God's Christ. Therefore it could be no accident.
It was not the mere outcome of Jewish opposition
and dislike. It was certainly divinely permitted
and designed. It was part of the deliberate
counsel of Almighty God. It was no catastrophe
forced upon and frustrating God's Will. It was
somehow carrying out and accomplishing that
Will. Moreover it is the death of the Sinless
One. Therefore it cannot be death for His own
sake, it must be for the sake of other people.

What then does the death of Jesus the Christ
and the Sinless really mean ? The answer to a
man of Saul's antecedents could not be mistaken.
Certainly that death means sacrifice. It is an
offering and a sacrifice to God, fragrant before Him
as the incense, acceptable in His sight. It is the
great offering of the Sinless on behalf of sin.
And Saul gathered all the best religious traditions of Israel to expound and explain that
death of the sinless Christ. He is the one Mediator
between God and man. God was in Christ reconciling the world unto Himself. This is the true
propitiation, which the conscience of Saul required,
but which he knew it was not within his power to
make. This is the reconciliation between earth
and Heaven.

For see : Christ Jesus is more than a mere solitary individual. He is the Divine ideal of all mankind. This is the perfection for which man was made. This is the realisation of man as he was meant to be in the days before God created him. This is man with his destiny achieved, man the reconciled, man the perfected. Christ is no mere individual. He is the Head of the human race. He is the second Adam. He is the first among many brethren. Where He is there He designs mankind to be. He is to bring many of the sons of men to glory. The perfection achieved in Him is by degrees to be also imparted to them. They are to become reconciled.

The only question is, How ?

S. Paul's answer is, There is not only Christ but there is *Christ's Kingdom* as well. Christ loved the Church and gave Himself for it. He has created by His Spirit a Community of the Redeemed. This kingdom of Christ is the sphere within which men are reconciled. It is the Body of Christ, and Christ Himself is the Head. Redemption was for S. Paul not simply an individual matter, it was a social thing. The individual was reconciled with God by being brought within the Kingdom or Church of the reconciled. Sinful mortals were thereby placed in Christ. And to be in Christ was to be a new creature.[1]

God was reconciled with the Church and therefore with every individual included within it. The Spirit of the glorified Christ works within the Church for the renewal of every sinful imperfect

[1] 2 Cor. v. 17.

character. S. Paul is conscious within himself
of new spiritual forces derived from Christ. He
is invigorated as never hitherto. He is another
man. Henceforth I live, yet not I but Christ
liveth in me. He is safe within the Kingdom of
the Reconciled. He knows himself to be reconciled, not for what he is but for what by the grace
of Christ he is to become. But he is accepted
already, here and now, by anticipation of the
effects which grace is to work in him. He has
won his heart's desire. He has received that
reconciliation which he could not secure for himself. There is therefore now no condemnation
to them that are in Christ Jesus.[1]

Can we not realise with what feelings of intense
relief Saul penned those words. He felt that God
had turned his heaviness into joy and girded him
with gladness. If Saul's modern critic dwells
upon the gloominess of this strange man of Tarsus
and his pessimistic views of religion, at any rate
Saul has become the optimist now. He goes about
the world singing and making melody in his heart
to the Lord. He is persuaded that nothing henceforth shall be able to separate him from the love
of God which is in Christ Jesus our Lord.

II

There are many thoughts which this sublime
experience crowds upon us. Let us select just
one or two.

  1. In modern times there are endlessly various
interpretations of Jesus. To one man He is the

[1] Rom. viii. 1.

sunny optimist of the Galilean lake, to another the inventor of inimitable stories and parables, to another the prophet, to another a great moralist, to another a teacher about God, to another the social reformer, to another a wonderful embodiment of what a human life should be.

But whatever truth is in these presentations, none of them separately, nor all of them together, could have satisfied S. Paul. For the simple reason that none of them bring reconciliation with God. There would have been no gospel to S. Paul in Jesus as master of paradox and unforgettable sentences.

The peculiar greatness and significance of S. Paul for Christianity consists in his capacity for insight into *principles*. He never lost his way among the details of the life of Christ. It was not that he had no interest in the details, but that he had a sense of proportion. He could appeal to a saying of Christ where necessary. He shows an allusive knowledge of many things in the earthly career.

But his own resistance to Christ, the peculiar bent of his genius, the way in which he came to be converted, all these forced him to go down to fundamental principles. He had to face the questions, Who Jesus is, for what does He stand ? What is it ultimately that He has done in the world and for all mankind ?

2. One final thought : it is this. Many persons to-day disparage theology as so much speculation and theory, and so much mere dogma, having very little to do with daily practical life. Theology, they say, is one thing, religion is another.

RECONCILIATION

Now of course it is true, painfully true, that it is possible to know a good deal of theology and yet to possess singularly little religion. But it is not also true that religion can get on without theology. On the contrary, religion without dogma is structure without foundation. Religion without theology becomes sentimental, vague, insecure, unable to stand the stress of life, and likely to fail us precisely in the very hour when we need it most.

Of this fact S. Paul is the standing witness. It is undeniable that his theology is the interpretation of his experience. It is the basis of his religion. Remove these dogmas of Jesus' Christhood, Sinless Perfection, and Redemptive work, and the whole of S. Paul's religious security and peace is also thereby ruined and destroyed. Religion for him is founded on theology. What Christ is and what Christ has done determines what the state of S. Paul's relationship to God can be.

We scarcely ought to close without reflecting on the personal lesson of this fact. If S. Paul is the great exponent of the doctrine of reconciliation with God through the death of Christ, it is because he is one of the greatest to know it as an experience. His theology and his religion go together.

It is of course too easy in our own case to divorce the two and to retain the theology without the religion. After all, is it a very profitable thing to know the process by which this wonderful man, almost two thousand years ago, came to be reconciled with his God, unless there is also something corresponding to it in our own religion ? It is so easy to substitute a speculative interest in theology for a personal experience of religion. May God in His infinite mercy grant that what we know as an intellectual theory, we may come to know as a living experience.

Mediation in the Jewish Religion

Mediation in the Jewish Religion[1]

'I stood between the Lord and you at that time.' DEUT. v. 8.

MODERN Judaism is remarkable for an emphatic rejection of the principle of mediation. Judaism, one of its authorities tells us, 'recognises in principle no mediatorship between God and Man.'

'Is it in the power of any human being to obtain forgiveness for the sin committed by his fellows?' asked the Chief Rabbi Hermann Adler.[2] And he gave the following reply:

Let us turn to a memorable incident recorded in the Bible. The wrath of the Almighty was roused against His people Israel, for they had set at nought His behests, and had made themselves an idol of gold, and worshipped it. Moses, deeply grieved, cries to the people, 'Ye have sinned a great sin, and now I will go up to the Lord; peradventure I will make an atonement for your sin.' The great leader was ready to sacrifice himself for his nation. He prays to God: 'Oh, this people have sinned a great sin, and made them gods of gold. Yet now if Thou wilt forgive their sin; and if not, blot me, I pray Thee, out of Thy book which Thou hast written.' Did the Lord accept this vicarious atonement? No. He said unto Moses: 'Whosoever has sinned against Me, him will I blot out from My book.' These words enunciate

---

[1] The writer would refer to a fuller treatment of this subject in the *Church Quarterly Review*, 1915.

[2] Adler, *Anglo-Jewish Memories*, 1904, pp. 243–4.

the doctrine that every man is accountable to God for his own actions, and cannot release himself from his individual responsibility by the intercession of another person, however great. We require no Mediator to save us from the effects of our guilt. Our own sincere repentance suffices to achieve for us Divine forgiveness.

Adler argued also from the doctrine of individual responsibility. Did not Ezekiel teach that every man should bear his own iniquities; that the son should not bear the iniquity of the father, neither the father the iniquity of the son?[1] To those who raised the objection: Was not the High Priest constituted on the Day of Atonement the representative of the people, who by his ministrations obtained the Divine pardon, so that he may be regarded as a mediator interceding between Israel and his God? Adler replied, 'If it had been in the power of the High Priest to achieve the forgiveness of the people, the Israelite would have been permitted on that day to pursue his ordinary occupation.'[2] The ministrations of the High Priest were clearly of no avail with the repentance of the people.[3]

Another authority, however, fully recognises that numerous examples of mediation occur in the Bible of the Jews. We naturally ask how the presence of such facts is to be accounted for. The answer of modern Judaism appears to be that 'the distance between Deity and frail humanity was too great to be overcome by the spiritual effort of the multitude or of the common individual. Hence the prophet, believed to be

[1] Adler, *Anglo-Jewish Memories*, 1904, p. 244.
[2] *Ibid.* p. 246.   [3] *Ibid.* p. 247.

in constant communion with God, is viewed in Scripture as the fit person to intercede on behalf of men in trouble.' [1]

I

Now clearly it is necessary here to consider first the Old Testament facts about mediation. It is necessary more or less to collect the evidence before we can estimate its worth. There are, it is acknowledged, many examples of the practice. They may be conveniently grouped in three divisions.

1. First, there is mediation in the general form of intercession. One of the grandest examples is the intercession of Abraham in behalf of the Cities of the Plain. ' The inhabitants of these cities were exceedingly wicked, so wicked that God thought it right to destroy them all. The story ran that this dread decision was revealed by God to Abraham.' [2] ' Abraham is represented as pleading with God for the deliverance of Sodom and Gomorrah if even but a few righteous men should be found within their walls.' [3]

Now the main features of this impressive incident are surely these. First, that Abraham is permitted to know of the impending judgment on the Cities of the Plain expressly because of his moral excellence and clearly in order that he should exercise that mediation for which his excellence qualified him. For the writer of this

[1] *Jewish Encyclopædia*, s.v. ' Mediator.'
[2] Montefiore, *The Bible for Home Reading*, i. 17.
[3] *Ibid.* p. 18.

story never supposed that the mediation of Abraham came unexpected to the Almighty, or that God was taken by surprise. On the contrary the opportunity is provided him. Then comes the Divine forbearance and the earnest pressure of the mediator, as six times over he pleads that the cities may be saved for the sake of the righteous few, until he has reduced the number lower and lower to the concession that the places shall be spared for the sake of ten.

2. There is also the mediation of the Covenant between God and Israel. Israel was to be ‘a peculiar treasure’ to God above all peoples, ‘a kingdom of priests and a holy nation.’ [1] But the Covenant was effected through the mediation of Moses. He was doubly constituted as mediator, both by the Divine appointment and also by the people’s desire. The messages from Heaven were given to Moses and through him communicated to Israel. ‘These are the words which thou shalt speak unto the children of Israel.’ [2] And on the other hand the people said, ‘Speak thou with us and we will hear : but let not God speak with us lest we die.’ [3] So ‘the people stood afar off and Moses drew near unto the thick darkness where God was.’ [4]

3. Thirdly, there is the mediation of the priest-hood. The entire Levitical system was one continuous mediation of the priesthood Godward for Israel. The priesthood occupied a necessary place in the devotional life of the chosen people.

---

[1] Exod. xix. 5–6.
[2] Exod. xx. 19.
[3] Exod. xix. 6.
[4] Exod. xx. 21.
[5] Deut. v. 5.

By them alone could certain functions be discharged. No layman in Israel was ever permitted to enter the Holy Place. There in the inner sanctuary which represented God's dwelling, God's immediate presence, stood no one but the High Priest. Upon his jewelled breastplate were inscribed the names of the Twelve Tribes. He bore the people on his heart to God. He stood there as their Divinely constituted representative achieving for them on the Day of Atonement that renewed reconciliation with God which it was his privilege alone to secure. Mediation then is the mark of Israel's worship, its characteristic through and through.

II

Now if these are the facts of mediation in the religion of Israel we are in a position to appreciate their worth. Modern Judaism admits the facts but denies their value. It ascribes their existence to inferior spirituality. They arose because ' the distance between Deity and frail humanity was too great to be overcome by the spiritual effort of the multitude or of the common individual.' [1]

It is natural to ask whether, if that were so in the great centuries which the Old Testament records, the condition of things is not much the same to-day. Is not humanity just as frail ? Is the common individual, to say nothing of the multitudes, more successful in spiritual effort than his predecessors in the Holy Land while the Temple was standing ?

[1] *Jewish Encyclopædia,* s.v. ' Mediator.'

RECONCILIATION

But whatever the answer to this may be it is difficult to see how mediation in Israel can be reasonably ascribed to unspirituality.

1. For consider who the mediators were. Abraham mediated for the cities of the plain, Moses for the restoration of Miriam, and for the forgiveness of the people. Samuel mediated for all Israel. Job offered sacrifice for his children's sins. Nehemiah confessed the sins of the children of Israel. Daniel did the same.[1]

Now all these are among Israel's best. They are among the most spiritually minded products of the Jew's religion. Is it easy to say that they were all engaged systematically in illustrating a principle which true Judaism excludes?

2. But that is not all. For this mediation was not a mere personal and private thing, introduced by unauthorised individuals into their private devotions. It was part of the official religion of Israel. It was deeply rooted in the religious system of the chosen people. The very covenant involved mediation. The sacrificial priesthood involved mediation. And these things were, from the Jewish point of view, no mere human devices. They were Divinely authorised. God Himself had directed them. How is it consistent with the traditional belief in the value of Israel's institutions to characterise mediation as a departure from the true principles of Israel's religion and a mark of spiritual inferiority?

[1] Neh. i. 7.

III

Let us now turn to some considerations on mediation in general.

1. We have found the objection raised that if mediation were true, the people for whom it was offered might have gone about their business, leaving the whole issue to their mediator. This is a curious misconception. Mediation is no substitute for personal effort. Let the offender exert all the efforts of which he is capable. Still, when he has done all this, may there not yet be room and need to supplement his efforts? And if this is the case even when he has done his best, is it not still more the case when his best is precisely what he has not done? Is not the general difficulty with the offender how to induce him to make that supreme exertion? Is it not true that the mediation of others between the offender and God, their Godward prayers and efforts in his behalf continually, are the very means whereby his personal efforts begin? Mediation is certainly not the same thing as personal effort, nor can it ever be a mere substitute for this. But does it follow that because mediation cannot do everything therefore it is no use? Surely this objection to the principle has not really been thought out. It would lead to such strange results on many things : results which no religious mind could possibly accept.

2. Then think of the bearing of mediation on our idea of Deity. Mediation was not founded on an imperfect idea of God. The Old Testament writers knew quite well that God was ever ready

to hear the sinners who repented. They knew
quite well that if Job pleaded for his children
God put it into his heart to plead. They knew
quite well that God was as deeply concerned
about the state of Israel as Nehemiah could be.
They never imagined that the wonderful pleading of Abraham for the sinful cities could be
interpreted as if Abraham was more merciful
than God. He knew perfectly that the Judge
of all the earth would certainly do right. It
was no secret to a Jew that if God put that
grace of intercession into His creature's mind,
the gift had not exhausted the generosity of
the Giver of the grace. The remonstrances of
Esdras form the most singularly impressive
proof of this. When the 'thoughts of his heart
were very grievous unto him, and he began to
talk with the Most High again,' [1] he did not
hesitate to reproach the Highest with the calamities
of Israel. He said that God out of all the trees
had chosen only one—the vine; and out of all
the flowers only one—the lily; and out of all
builded cities—Sion; and yet His one chosen
people God had now forsaken. 'Why hast Thou
given this one people over unto many? . . .
If Thou didst so much hate Thy people, yet
shouldest Thou punish them with Thine own
hands.'

So the prophet exhausts himself in his grief
and his reproaches. And the Most High hears
His servant in silence. And then when the
reproaches cease, comes the calm and gentle
answer : 'Thou art sore troubled in mind for

[1] 2 Esdras v. 23.

Israel's sake : lovest thou that people better than He that made them ? '

The intercessor is evidently deeply moved and quieted. 'I said, No, Lord; but of my grief have I spoken : for my reins pain me every hour, while I labour to comprehend the way of the Most High and seek out part of His judgment.'

Thus Israel recognised the dignity and the value of intercession. It found a real place in religion for the principle of mediation.

3. We have found that there are some to whom the idea of mediation seems irreconcilable with the fact of personal responsibility. Now personal responsibility is indeed a fact impossible to be gainsaid. Ezekiel has formulated it for all ages when he declared that the son shall not bear the iniquity of the father, nor the father the iniquity of the son; that it is the soul which sins that is the soul which shall die, or bear the punishment of its own sin. But true as all this is, surely it is after all only one aspect of the truth. There is no such thing as a vicarious punishment. That is true. Nevertheless there is such a thing as vicarious suffering. If there is a personal responsibility there is a social responsibility also. And Israel realised the social truth as well as the individual. The reception of grace and blessings through the community of the Covenant was no strange thought for Israel.

There are two ways in which it is possible to regard the sins of other people. One is to say that it is entirely their own concern. Their sin is between themselves and their Maker. It is their business, for they have done it. It is not

I

ours. And we may proceed to support our view with the scriptural quotation that every man must bear his own burden.

A little reflection, however, may lead us to perceive that, however true this is, there is another side as well; and that if one scripture affirms our individual responsibility, there is another which enjoins the duty of bearing one another's burdens. If we lived every separate soul in a planet by ourselves then the theory of our moral insularity might be sufficient for the circumstances. But we are not isolated units, and cannot be explained that way. We are members of a family, of a nation, of a race. And therefore it is morally impossible not to be concerned about other people's transgressions.

In the family, when one member sins, the reflection is at times inevitable that if the other members had been better, wiser, more considerate, less self-centred, perhaps the evil might never have been. There is the solemn thought that our own defects may partially account for, though of course they cannot justify, other people's sins. But, even apart from that, no man liveth unto himself. The honour of one member is the honour of all the house. And the dishonour of the one casts its shadow upon all. We cannot help being concerned about the honour or the dishonour of our homes.

In the nation the same thing holds. There is the responsibility of the community as a whole towards the members of the same. There is the consciousness that the wrongdoings of the individual may be partly accounted for by his disadvantages. The more happily placed should be constrained to reflect on the less fortunate : if he had had my opportunities he might have done far better ; if I had had his drawbacks I might have done far worse. But quite apart from that sense of sympathy, there is the unquestionable fact that the ill-doings of the individual are and must be the concern of the whole community. For he disqualifies himself thereby for the service which otherwise he could render. Either he contributes to elevate the moral standard of the community or else he contributes to bring it down.

Consequently a man is bound to be concerned about other people's sins, because he is bound to be interested in the moral welfare of the community. He is bound to do something if he can to neutralise the effect. And this is the moral motive for philanthropy. He may not be in the least religious. He may not even believe that God exists. But he is quite sure that the nation does. And he feels bound to contribute to the uplifting of the community. And he cannot do that without being concerned about other people's sins.

Now if a man is not only moral but also religious then there enters in a still higher consideration. For now he has not only to be concerned with the interests of humanity, he has also to be concerned with the interests of God. For he recognises that God has the supreme claim upon all human powers, upon the nation's loyalty and devotion. Whatever else it serves it is to serve God first. Now the sins of other people are not only wrongs inflicted on the interests of humanity, they are

also wrongs inflicted upon the honour of God.
And he, the individual, has enlisted in the service
of God. Now it is impossible to serve God without
caring for God's honour. Therefore he must be
distressed for the wrong inflicted upon that honour
by the sins of other people. But, it will be said,
he himself has inflicted wrongs upon that same
Divine honour. Yes: no doubt he has. And it
does profoundly affect and compromise a man's
concern for the wrong inflicted on God by others
to remember that he has wronged the honour of
God himself. This fact sobers and humbles him
and fills him with the sense of his own complete
unworthiness to be concerned with God's interests
at all. Nevertheless he cannot escape the obliga-
tions of his position. His Godward loyalty compels
his Godward sorrow for the sins of other men.
He cannot truly be God's servant, on the Lord's
side, unless he does this thing.

And it is profoundly true that in the confession
of other people's sins to God there enters a new experience and a closer relationship with God. To
approach Him in sorrow for self is to be conscious
of distance and restraint. To approach Him in
sorrow for the sins of someone else is to be brought
in a deeper way more closely on God's side. It
is to be identified more intimately with God's
interests, and in a more disinterested way. The
priest who has sorrowed before God for the sins
of some penitent soul, the mother who has in deep
distress sorrowed before God for the sin of her
child, know how true this is.

4. In point of fact if we are to exclude mediation
from religion we must exclude intercession. For

intercession is nothing else than the Godward intervention of one person on behalf of another. Now plainly it is impossible to exclude intercession. But to admit it is to admit the principle of mediation. Every parent who has pleaded Godward for a child, every person who has prayed for a friend, could say with perfect truth as Moses said, I stood between the Lord and you at that time: so deeply rooted is mediation into the very constitution of human life. Every man, every woman, every child, is or may become a mediator.

IV

The attempt to exclude mediation from modern Judaism and to apologise for its acknowledged existence in their sacred books, is supremely important in the relation between Judaism and Christianity. For it is an obvious thing that those who find no need of mediation will not readily appreciate a religion which is fundamentally the religion of mediation. The whole redemptive work of Christianity is founded on the principle of mediation. So long, therefore, as Judaism recoils from mediation so long it must repudiate the Church of Christ.

The advocates of Judaism are well aware of this. Rejection of mediation is an effective precaution against the advance of Christianity. If mediation is unspiritual, a concession to moral weakness, then the religion which of all others is founded upon that principle is inferior and self-condemned. But if antagonism to mediation is controversially advantageous, may there not easily be unconscious danger of prejudicial treatment of this principle ? It is certainly a singular feature of the modern situation that Christians should be appealing to Jews to set a higher value on a conspicuous element of their own Scriptures.

Is it not also worth reflecting whether the modern Jewish depreciation of the mediatory element in their Bible is not partly due to the age-long cessation of the Levitical priestly work ? If to-day, as in the days of old, the Jew saw enacted before his eyes the propitiation embodied in sacrifice and in the intercessions of the Hebrew priest, would it not be far more difficult for him to depreciate the use of mediation ? It is easier to depreciate that which is obsolete than that which forms the living ritual, the *lex orandi*, of one's religion. After well-nigh two thousand years have elapsed since the sacrifice was offered in the sanctuary of Jerusalem, since altar or priesthood existed, it is natural that many a Jew should look on that form of mediation as something which has for ever passed away. But we are bound to plead that for a Jew at any rate the sanction of that form of mediation is nothing less than Divine ; and moreover, if the special form has ceased, the principle underlying it is abiding. And certainly that school of modern Judaism which aspires to the restoration of the Temple services is in reality pledged to value the principle of mediation. Meanwhile that principle is so deeply rooted in the spiritual necessities of human nature that no religion which neglects or omits it can satisfy the claim to be the perfect form of religion for mankind.

The Principle of Reparation

The Principle of Reparation[1]

'Wherewith shall I come before the Lord ? ' MICAH vi. 6.

THERE is a deeply-rooted human instinct that when a wrong has been done some sort of reparation ought to be made. This is manifest in every department of human experience.

It is found in the legal sphere. We are all familiar with the law of compensation and the notion of damages. It is found in the moral sphere. Every child can understand that when he has been unkind and inconsiderate he ought to be particularly kind and considerate to make amends for the hurt he has inflicted. And the thought is still more self-evident for the mature. Whether it takes the form of restitution in cases which law does not reach, or sacrifice of selfish preferences in cases which a higher morality dictates, the principle of reparation is one of world-wide recognition.

It is found in the religious sphere. It runs through all religions. It takes crude forms with primitive faiths, where the conception of the character of Deity is low. It becomes stern and tragic as religions proceed. It developed and matured in Israel as the moral sublimity of God became better understood. The whole religious worship of Israel was one long effort at reparation. It was consummated in Christianity. For Christendom took its conception of God from the revelation of Christ. And Christ's revelation of

---

[1] Preached at St. Saviour's, Eastbourne. Lent, 1915.

God, given in Christ's teaching, Christ's character, and Christ's experience, was a revelation of inexorable rectitude as well as of boundless compassion ; it forced the mind to contemplate the goodness and the severity of God. Consequently it strengthened man's belief in the necessity of religious reparation.

I

The question, therefore, which immediately arises is the profoundly practical one : Who is to make the reparation ? And, of course, the natural and obvious answer may be given that the person who is to make the reparation is and must be the person who committed the offence. Consider, then, reparation as made by the person who did the wrong.

Now, before we proceed any distance at all in this direction what impresses us is the inadequacy of much that goes by the name of reparation.

For instance, in the legal sphere we get a money compensation for an insulted honour. Thus we put in one scale so much insulted honour, and in the other so much cash. But who can seriously consider the two to be equivalent ? The whole conception of a financial compensation for a moral offence is from a moral standpoint simply preposterous. Whatever a legal fiction may profess, there is in such a transaction no reparation made. And if inadequacy is the mark of legal compensation, the case is even worse in the moral sphere. Let us take an extreme example. There is a certain home : the mother and the children are there, but the father is not. It is true that he maintains them, in a way; but he has not crossed that threshold for some years. She is left to bear the burden, unhelped, uncomforted. If he shall one day return, and take his place in his own home, to find defects in the children which he might have prevented, no love for him in the hearts of his own children, to whom he is no more than a stranger: what possible reparation will it be in his power to make? This instance is extreme. But the impossibility of reparation is not only in such an instance as this. It is piteously far extended through human life. When to the session of silent thought we summon up remembrance of things past, and vanished faces reappear in the chambers of our imagination, too often we have cause to contemplate with pain the hardness, even the heartlessness, which we inflicted on our own. We may wonder what cross devil prompted us to act that way. We may gnaw our hearts out with remorse at the recollection of departed scenes. We may be stung and goaded into a self-discipline unknown to us before. We may be deepened, and never be the same that once we were. But the one thing we cannot do is this: we cannot make an adequate reparation.

Now, if this is the fact that insufficiency is the mark of all the reparation between man and man, is it not much more the case when the reparation is between man and God?

The ancient Jewish prophet felt all this, and felt it most acutely.[1]

He sets before his mind, in an ascending scale

[1] Micah vi. 6 and 7, Revised Version.

of costliness, the possible offerings that he can make to God in reparation for his own transgressions. He feels that none of them, nor all of them together, could be any real equivalent for the wrong he has done in God's world. He clearly sees that transgression is a deeper thing than to admit of any external compensation. And even when the external offering becomes, as it does in the offering of his own son, the costliest that can be conceived, the outward sign of the inward self-surrender; yet, in the depth of his moral insight, he is clear that even this can be no adequate reparation for moral wrong.

In truth the problem of reparation is one which the prophet cannot solve. He proceeds, indeed, with the beautiful reply:

'He hath showed thee, O man, what is good; and what doth the Lord require of thee, but to do justly, and to love mercy, and to walk humbly with thy God?'

But this is no help whatever to the conscience painfully aware that this doing justly is exactly what the offender has not done. To tell a man burdened with a sense of his transgressions what it is that the Lord his God requires, is certainly no solution of the problem which confronts an awakened and anxious soul. The cry of the sensitive conscience is: 'Wherewith shall I come before the Lord?' And that problem remained, for the deepest and best in Israel, unanswerable.

And this insufficiency in the character of all human reparation to God becomes more deeply and impressively convincing if we analyse the offender's moral state. No doubt the offender could make true reparation if only his repentance could be perfect. But this is exactly what it is not. Can I ever induce myself to think that my poor apology is an adequate reparation for the wrong which I have done to God? for what I have wrought within His moral world? Is it not painfully true that the serious mind must constantly complain: 'I know that I ought to be more sorry than I am'? Is it not often said that it is much if our repentance itself does not need to be repented of? But even when the repentance of the offender is at its best, it is the effort of a character clouded and compromised by sin. It is the effort of a will enfeebled by its own unfaithfulness. Thus it is a self-judgment disabled by its own past. No man can at the same moment be poisoned by his own act, and yet free in his moral system from the assimilated evil. Hence it is terribly true, as we have been so ably reminded by Moberly,[1] that it is impossible for the sinner perfectly to repent.

This is no new discovery. Deeply religious men have often felt its truth. Years ago the evangelical writer Alexandre Vinet recorded it in the following expression: 'Convinced that the violated moral order imperiously exacts a reparation that I had not the power to offer.'[2] That conviction is surely profoundly true. It is a phrase which has burnt itself in upon the memory. It is a record of the deepest insight. There, confronting us, is the moral order violated. And

---

[1] Moberly, *Atonement and Personality*.
[2] *Life of Vinet*, by Lane, p. 79.

it is impossible for the offender to make adequate reparation.

What, then, is to be done? Must God take the best He can get, and put up with the inadequacy? Can we believe this is possible? If the inadequate reparation which the sinful can make is all that will ever be offered before God, then no real reparation will ever be made for the sin of the world. Is that possible? Would it not, then, appear that the victory remained with sin? Surely we are constrained to look for reparation. The cry of humanity is : 'Wherewith shall I come before the Lord?' Wherewith? That is the question. And, apart from Christianity, that problem remains, and must remain, unsolved.

II

Reparation by the offender has failed. We come, then, to the answer of Christianity. It is that the perfect reparation is made by One who had no share whatever in the wrong.

Reparation is made by the sinless Christ. Now, the sinlessness of Christ implies a capacity for perfect sorrow over human sin. For sinlessness means exemption from all influences by which the moral judgment is disqualified. He knew by experience what moral freedom meant. He saw around Him a race which was morally enslaved. He therefore was able to offer to the Father a perfect sorrow for the sin of the world.

Now, of course, the obvious criticism on this is that it is sheer substitution. One person does the wrong, and another does the reparation.

THE PRINCIPLE OF REPARATION

But in answer it must be remembered that this principle of vicarious reparation pervades all human life, and pervades it through and through. Reparation of wrong by those who had no share in the wrong is one of the most constant of human experiences. It follows as a necessity upon the social and corporate constitution of mankind. For mankind is not a multitude of isolated units. It is a race, an organism, a community. It reaps the consequences of its own deeds collectively. It makes collective reparation. Have we not seen it in numerous instances? Augustine sins, and Monica makes reparation. Job makes reparation for the sins of his children; the Jewish patriot for the sins of his people.

Here is a fresh illustration. It is in modern life. There is a certain Home where children are rescued who have been wronged by the cruelty of mankind. There, environed by kindness and by faith, they are helped, if possible, to forget the past, and to begin their life afresh. If one of those who injured them should take a walk and pass that way, and ask, 'What place is this?' he surely might be told, 'This is a Home of Reparation. You did the wrong. We make the reparation.' And that reparation is not only offered to the child or to the human race beyond the child; it is offered also to the child's Creator, to the Lord God of love and compassion on high. That is the principle of vicarious reparation.

Now, Christ is self-identified with all mankind. He is not only human, and the ideal man, and therefore representative; but He is lovingly self-identified with the human race. In Christ the heavenly Father heard something entirely new upon the earth. It was a human voice pronouncing perfect judgment on human sin; perfectly concurring in the judgment of the Father upon sin; gathering up, and fusing into one, and perfecting, all the earth's imperfect reparations; and offering a perfect sorrow for the sin of the world. And in that loving sorrow, perfectly self-identified with the cause of humanity, and higher still with the cause of God in humanity, He went to the last surrender possible, which is the surrender of death. 'Greater love hath no man than this, that a man lay down his life for his friends.' And in this He consummated His reparation. It was neither the form of His death nor the fact of His death in which the reparation lay; but in the spirit and in the moral purpose for which He yielded up His life.

And then, viewed on the other side, this reparation does not mean that Christ sorrowed and therefore I need not; that Christ made the reparation, I have no more to do. That would be sheer travesty of the Christian truth. If Christ is self-identified with us, we also are to become self-identified with Christ. Each one of us must come to think Christ's thoughts after Him. We are to say, in effect: 'This is the sorrow which my sin requires and my conscience attests. This is the reparation which ought to be, but which I could not make. With that sorrow, with that reparation, I will identify myself, so far as my moral cloudiness permits. I will crave to be accepted in the Beloved, that is, in union with the perfections of His glorious reparation; following with my feeble, faltering sorrow the realities of His tremendous sorrow, in which He has enfolded me, and which took away the sin of all the world.'

And, if there is one thing certain, it is that nothing in the whole religious experience of mankind has so deepened and intensified the capacity of the sinful to make a Godward reparation as this reparation offered by the sinless Christ.

Christ is God's greatest Gift to man. And when the Father gave us Christ, He furnished humanity with the means of making its own Godward reparation.

III

This is, as I believe, the Christian doctrine of reparation. And, looking back upon it, I would lay stress on the sublime idea it gives concerning God, and on the deep idea it gives concerning sin. It teaches that God does not simply forgive without an effort, as some wealthy man might give us what he will not miss, nor overlook our sins like some indulgent parent more conspicuous for gentleness than for moral strength. On the contrary, it insists that the rectification of the moral disorders of the world is a costly thing; that the sin of man invades the very being of Deity; that it presents a problem, so to say, even for God Himself; that it involved the sacrifice of His only Son; that, while He devised a means to bring His banished home, He caused the perfect reparation to be made in man for man by Man, even by the Man whom He Himself had constituted and chosen.

Now, I am deeply sure that it is not when I am at my worst, but when I am at my best, that this wonderful conception appeals to me the most. In all the religions of the world, so far as these doctrines have come my way, I know no theory of reparation which comes within measurable distance of this. And if our highest thoughts are nearest to reality, then must this Christian conception have the chiefest right to the acceptance of men, because it must be the message of the truth.

The Heavenly Priesthood
of Christ

The Heavenly Priesthood of Christ

'Thou art a Priest for ever.' HEB. vii. 17.

IT is clear that much may be learnt of a religion from the construction of its house of prayer. Now the sanctuary of Israel consisted of two parts. There was the open court, a vast quadrangle with cloisters round. And in the midst of the open court the sacred house. The court was large, the house was small. In the open court the congregation assembled. But the sacred house they never entered. There it stood isolated and veiled from human gaze. The meaning of this construction is obvious. The open court represented earth. The sacred house represented Heaven. Here in the one men might assemble and pray. There in the other dwelt God the Unapproachable. The Jews' profound belief in the awful holiness shows itself deeply cut into the very construction of their sanctuary. The way into the holiest place was not yet plain. Sinful mankind must remain without.

Now the work of the priest and the form of the sanctuary correspond. Part of his duty lay in the outer court and part in the sacred house. The devotion of Israel was consummated in the service of the great Day of Atonement which was the yearly act of national propitiation of God for the sins of the people. On that day the high priest began his work in the outer court.

RECONCILIATION

There, in the face of all the people, at the great altar, the sacrifice was slain. This was the beginning of the offering : but it was no more. It was essential of course that the victim should die. But if the priest had ended there the propitiation would not have been achieved. Now came the second part of the priestly work : that for which the death prepared the way. The priest now took the blood of the sacrifice, and with it he approached the sacred house. With every token of reverence, and conscious that he was not fit, he now passed within the hangings which veiled the sacred dwelling, and disappeared from the sight of the congregation. There, as every instructed Jew would know, he sprinkled the blood of the sacrifice upon the mercy seat and before the mercy seat seven times.[1] Now this sprinkling of the blood within the holiest place was the act of reconciliation. It is called reconciling the Holy Place. It is an act in the immediate presence of the holy God. It is an offering of the blood within the holiest place. The priest 'offered it for himself and for the errors of the people.'[2] He purified the sacred house, God's dwelling-place, from the defilement caused by Israel's transgressions.

Thus the high priest represented repentant Israel. There he stood in the holiest in Israel's behalf. God and Israel through this propitiation were reconciled.

[1] Lev. xvi. 14. [2] Heb. ix. 7.

II

Now, says the writer to the Hebrews, keep all this religious ceremonial before your minds, and then turn to contemplate the work of Christ. For it is in terms of this ceremonial that His work can be explained. Think of Christ as priest and His work will be clear to you.

Consider what is a priest? Here is the writer's definition.[1] A priest is an individual taken from among men; appointed for men in things pertaining to God; that he may offer both gifts and sacrifices for sins. That is to say, a human being, appointed in man's behalf for a Godward work, that work being the offering of sacrifice. He is also one who is not self-constituted but divinely authorised and commissioned.

All that is exactly what Christ is.

Reconciliation as wrought in Israel was imperfect in every way.[2] It was imperfect, because the priesthood was imperfect, and because the sacrifice was imperfect. The priesthood was an order of sinful men, a mere series of sinful units who did their office and passed away.

The sacrifice was imperfect. It was an involuntary offering of a beast which could not understand, and upon whom by a mere fiction the sins of the people were symbolically laid.

It was impossible that this ceremonial propitiation should take away sins. It was a succession of separate sacrifices. Year after year a new offering was brought. A fact which demonstrated the insufficiency of the offerings previously made.

[1] Heb. v. 1. [2] See Nairne, *The Epistle of Priesthood*, p. 140.

Consequently the priesthood in Israel gives a most imperfect idea of the priesthood of Christ. For He was immeasurably superior in every way. And the author of the Hebrews looks round for a more suitable illustration. There occurs to him the figure of Melchizedek. There it was already in the mystic line of the Psalm. 'Thou art a priest for ever after the order of Melchizedek.'

Here was the figure of a priest whose entrance and disappearance alike were involved in mystery. His name denotes king of righteousness and his office denotes king of peace. He stands in no line of succession. He is not one of a series, but simply is by himself unique. He represents the notion of continuous and abiding priesthood and offering. Let us take him therefore, says the author, as an illustration of the priesthood of Christ.

Not that we are to forget the priesthood in Israel, but rather to supplement its deficiencies by the spiritual ideas suggested in the priesthood of Melchizedek.

What we are to realise then about the priesthood of Christ may be put in three words :

It is permanent.

It is universal.

It is moral and not merely ceremonial.

We come then to consider Christ's high priestly work. The Epistle to the Hebrews parallels Christ's work as priest with the double action of the Jewish high priest on the Day of Atonement. The two parts of the priestly work in Israel correspond to the two parts of the priestly work of Christ. Just as the Levitical high priest discharged his propitiatory duties partly at the altar and partly in the holiest place, so Christ wrought His propitiation partly on earth and partly in Heaven. As the Levitical high priest stood by the altar where the sacrificial victim was slain, so Christ was slain upon the altar of the Cross. As the Levitical high priest offered the blood of the sacrifice as an act of propitiation within the holiest place, so Christ offered His own Blood in the presence in Heaven.

1. First, then, is the priesthood of Christ on earth. On earth is the death of Christ. The offering must of necessity be slain. 'Apart from shedding of blood there is no remission.' [1] It is the sacrifice of Himself. The sinless priest must pass through death.

2. But this priesthood of Christ on earth is only the beginning, the opening stage, the preliminary, to His priesthood in Heaven. It is almost startling to notice how quickly the sacred writer hastens on from Christ's work on earth to Christ's work in Heaven. For Him the work on earth is of course essential, but essential as a preparation for something else. It makes the priestly work in Heaven possible. It provides the life which has passed through death. It provides the offering which Christ can present in Heaven.

Thus the whole interest of the sacred writer is concentrated on the priesthood in Heaven, just as the interest of a Jew was concentrated on the propitiation wrought by their high priest in the Holy Place.

[1] Heb. ix. 22.

Christ then by His ascension enters as the Great High Priest into Heaven itself. He 'enters in once for all into the Holy Place having obtained eternal redemption.' [1]

He has entered into the Heavens, there to appear in the presence of God in our behalf. He is reconciling the Holy Place. He was not only a priest while He wrought on earth. He is more than ever a priest now that He resides in Heaven.

There are modern Christians who appear to think that Christ was only a priest so long as He lived on earth. That is an opinion which cannot be reconciled with the Epistle to the Hebrews, nor held without cancelling the main principles which that book of Scripture contains. No, our Lord did not retire from office at the ascension. On the contrary, He is still High Priest now that He has entered Heaven. There in Heaven an essential part of His work remains to be done.

He is a priest for ever.

III

The value of this interpretation of Christ's redemptive work in terms of priesthood is extremely great. It is one aspect of the Apostolic teaching. If the preference of other schools of thought would lead them to interpret Christ as prophet or else as king, it still remains unalterably true that one of the New Testament authorities thought fit to interpret Him as priest. It cannot be right to evade this fact if we would share the primitive Christian belief. It will never do to

[1] Heb. ix. 12.

say that this was done only by one author; as if the frequency of recurrence were the only test of a doctrine's truth. The question is not merely how often it occurs. The fact remains that it is there. Nor will it do to say that this was done to suit a special class of readers at that date. However correct that statement may be, it does not alter the fact that to one of the Scriptural writers the interpretation of Christ's redemptive work in terms of priesthood was good and true.

The Perpetual Offering
of Christ

The Perpetual Offering
of Christ [1]

IF the Eucharistic Offering is to be appreciated rightly it must not be propounded by itself, but in relation to the facts and principles by which it was created.

Much harm is done by proposing it in isolation. For it will be found that those who reject it base their rejection on a certain view of Christ's redemptive work. It is, therefore, with that redemptive work that it is necessary to begin.

I

First, then, we contemplate the Offering on the Cross. It is part of the faith of a Christian that we were redeemed by Christ's death. Scripture lays the greatest stress upon that death. 'We were redeemed by the precious Blood of Christ as of a lamb without blemish and without spot.' 'Thou hast redeemed us unto God by Thy Blood.'

1. Now beyond all doubt the particular form of death which Christ endured is the most affecting and constraining appeal that could be made to the heart of mankind. We know and feel most deeply that this is true. And yet if our Lord had died what we call a natural death in His own house in Capernaum, with His disciples around Him and His mother by His side, in the calm of the

---

[1] Preached in Chelmsford Cathedral on Ascension Day, 1915.

evening while the darkness fell on the waters of Galilee, He would not have appealed to the conscience of humanity with the same effect, but He would none the less have redeemed the world. What I mean is that it was not so much the form of His death but the death itself which redeemed. Crucifixion was not a Jewish but a Roman penalty. It was the fusion of the two nationalities which rendered it historically possible. Of course the fusion, like all the preparation for Christ, was providential. Thus the actual form of the death was assuredly no accident, but part of the determined counsel and foreknowledge of God. It was the form of redemption divinely and determinedly selected. Yet none the less it was not the form, but the death itself which actually redeemed.

2. Yet further still. If it was not the form of the death which redeemed, neither was it the death itself considered as mere fact. So long as that death is considered merely as externally inflicted by the Roman power at the instigation of the Jews, there is nothing about it which redeems. Redemption does not lie in the mere fact that Jesus died, but in the motive, the intention, the purpose, with which He accepted that death and endured it. The redeeming power of the death consists in death accepted in the spirit of reparation. It is the moral not the mere physical which redeems. The physical death was but the outward expression of the deep inward surrender of the very self to the honour and glory of the All-holy Father.

Hence it is true to say that we are redeemed more by Christ's sorrow than by Christ's death.

Important consequences ensue. For the redeeming sorrow of Christ did not begin upon the cross. The trial, the scourging, must be included in the redemptive work. So also must Gethsemane. So also must the institution of the Eucharist. So also must the entire matured reflective manhood of our Lord, from the day, whenever it was, that the full meaning of His redemptive mission confronted and took possession of His human mind, form part of His redemption of the world. It is by His will that we are saved. Redemption did not begin upon the cross.

Neither did it end when the cross was over. Our Lord upon the cross said indeed, ' It is finished.' But we must be careful to understand precisely what it was that was finished. The physical pain was finished. The earthly career was finished. The dying and the death were almost finished. He had finished all that He came into the world to do. But the spirit of reparation was not finished. That is, and in the nature of things must be, continuous. Redemption consists in the entire moral attitude of Christ. The outward expressions, even the greatest, of that spirit might come and go, but that spirit of reparation abides in perpetuity.

II

This naturally leads us on to our second leading theme, which is the offering in Heaven.

1. If we ask, Where is Jesus now ? the answer of course will be given, He is in Heaven. And if we ask the further question, What is He doing there ? some people would reply, He is resting

from His labours; He has finished His work; He is now reaping His reward. Scripture will very probably be quoted confirming this: ' This Man, after He had offered one sacrifice for sins for ever, sat down on the right hand of God.' To this will be added the language of the Creed: ' He ascended into heaven, and sitteth at the right hand of God the Father Almighty.' The redemption, then, is regarded as achieved. There is nothing more remaining to be done.

But, then, if you were to remark, Does not the Bible also say that Christ has gone to appear in the presence of God in our behalf; and that He ever liveth to make intercession for us ? you find not infrequently that this intercession of Christ in heaven is either entirely ignored or else explained as a mere reference to the past historic fact of Calvary. It is suggested that Christ is in reality seated at the right hand of God, but that He does not in reality intercede.

Now, I submit that this treatment of the Scripture teaching is not right. For since the Scripture tells us two things so different concerning Christ, as that He is seated at the right hand of God and also that He intercedes, we have absolutely no right whatever to efface the one by the aid of the other. Rather our business is to give to each idea its proper place, and to regard them both as real aspects of Christ's life in heaven.

What, then, is meant by the expression, ' Christ sat down at the right hand of God ' ? Plainly the language must be figurative, for the simple reason that it cannot possibly be taken literally. There is no such thing as the right hand of God.

For God is pure Spirit. The only question therefore is, What can these words denote? The right
hand of God means exaltation; it means glory,
blessedness, and power. And the service of Christ
at God's right hand means His continued possession of that glory and blessedness. It represents
Christ's close proximity to the Father; Christ's
glorified state.

Now, what is meant by the other phrase,
' He ever liveth to make intercession for us '?
It may be perfectly true that these words are not
to be taken literally any more than the former
words; that they do not necessarily mean that
Christ is engaged in Heaven in a verbal repetition
of the prayer upon the cross, ' Father, forgive
them; for they know not what they do.' But
the words must certainly not be explained away.
The intercession of Christ in heaven is just as
real as His intercession on the cross. That is
to say, His pleading for mankind did not cease
upon His death. On the contrary, Christ's intercession is a continuous intercession. It is
perpetuated at the right hand of the Father, in
the glory of the Father, even now. Nay, more:
' He ever liveth to make intercession.' This is
the express purpose for which He is there. Intercession is the peculiar work of the glorified Christ.
It is this upon which His redemptive activities
are engaged. In a hymn written some years ago
upon the Passion the line occurs, ' Jesus the
Crucified pleads for me.' That line has been
adversely criticised on the ground that we cannot
tell that the human mind of Jesus was concerned
with each single soul during the few hours He

hung upon the cross. This criticism no doubt is true. Christ's intercession on the cross was primarily concerned with the men who crucified Him. It may be extended to all His contemporaries, and then to the range of the entire human race from first to last. But it was concerned with them collectively, with humanity as a whole, rather than with the separate units and their separate needs. May we not say that what He did for men collectively on the cross He does for them individually now in heaven? At this very hour, Christ in the glory of the Father, in the heavenly blessedness, is engaged in interceding one by one for the men and women now in the struggles of life. As, long ago, He said to Peter, ' I have prayed for thee that thy faith fail not '; so now He might say to any one of us, ' I intercede for thee individually, and thy special needs.' Surely that is a thought which is of the highest value to-day. Was there ever a time in the world's history when the intercession of Christ was more significant, more required? Is it not full of consolation and power? We are not concerned simply with the historic Jesus Who interceded almost two thousand years ago, but with the living Christ in the glory of the Father Who is interceding now. The collective intercession of the cross is continued in the individual intercession in Heaven.

2. Secondly, to the heavenly intercession must be added the heavenly priesthood of Christ.

Recall as briefly as possible the picture which the Epistle to the Hebrews drew : how it pointed to the priesthood in Israel as a great illustration of the redemptive work of Christ. How it enforced the distinction between priestly work on earth and in Heaven. How the symbolism of the Jewish sanctuary was utilised to explain the two main parts of the priestly work of Christ. How the Jewish high priest, on the great atoning day, stood by the altar in the outer court, which represented earth, while the victim was being slain. How this action at the altar at the outer court, essential though it was, yet only prepared the way for the reconciliation yet to be. How the Jewish high priest then entered on his greater and higher work. How he went up into the holiest place, and there consummated the reconciliation in the very presence of God. How the devotion of the worshipping throng was concentrated, not on the death in the outer court but rather on the offering in the holy place. How all that Jewish symbolism, imperfect though it was, shadowy though it was, and inadequate for the supreme purpose of reconciling earth and heaven, nevertheless is a true illustration of the priestly work of Christ. How just as the Levitical high priest stood at the altar in the outer court while the victim was slain, so Christ the true High Priest was slain upon the altar of the cross. How just as the victim's death in the Jewish ceremonial was but preliminary to the offering of the victim's blood, so the death of Christ was but preliminary to the offering which He had yet to make in Heaven. How just as the Jewish high priest passed through into the holiest place, and made the reconciliation there, so Christ, the true High Priest, completed His reconciliation in Heaven.

How the Lord's ascension is the entrance of the great High Priest into the holiest sphere. How He has gone into Heaven, there to appear in the presence of God in our behalf. How the priesthood of Christ is not so much on earth as it is in Heaven. How the attention of Christian devotion is concentrated rather on that heavenly priesthood than on Christ's work on earth. For the work on earth, essential as it is, was consummated by the priesthood of Christ in Heaven. How every priest must have somewhat to offer, and how Christ is offering there in the glory of the Father. How the ascension means priesthood in Heaven. How that priesthood is a permanent enduring thing, so long as human need shall last. For Christ is a priest for ever.

3. Thirdly, let us think of the heavenly offering. It is impossible to separate Christ's offering from Christ. He is not one and His offering another. For the offering which He made and makes is Himself. The offering and the Offerer are one. It consists of the entire spirit of reparation. This is the essence of the redemption. And that spirit of reparation, while it can be expressed in an outward experience, is in itself a continuous and abiding state. It is a moral condition. Wherever Christ is, He is full of the spirit of reparation. Nay, Christ is the permanent embodiment of reparation in its perfect state. That is the spirit which dominates Him now in Heaven as much as ever it did when He was on earth. Christ does not point the Father back to Calvary as an offering completed in the past. The perfect man is now in the Father's presence, a human

being who has passed through death, and who in virtue of that experience is more matured, more qualified now than ever He was on earth, for consummating the work of reconciliation. For surely it is true of human nature always, that when it passes transfigured into that higher state, it becomes more capable of spiritual things than ever before. And this universal experience must be true also of the perfect Man. He was matured and ripened, sinless though He was, through the experiences 'in the days of His flesh.' [1] Our 'great High Priest,' Who has 'passed into the heavens,' is now more than ever, if that be possible, 'touched with the feeling of our infirmities.' [2] It is as qualified by earth's experience that He is become, in the fullest sense, our great High Priest. There is in heaven 'a Lamb as it had been slain': One Who has passed through death and beyond it; One Who is the perfect spirit of reparation, now, at this very hour, in the presence of God.

Thus it is true to say that the world's redemption was not necessarily completed in three hours, no, nor in three centuries, no, nor even in well-nigh two thousand years. It is a continuous process of reparation perpetuated in the spirit of Christ to the end of time. Or rather, it cannot be measured by the tests of time at all. For it is the heart and will of Christ ; the abiding state of His perfect Humanity.

To contemplate redemption merely as a great event, ever receding more and more into the inaccessible distances, is to inflict on real religion a grievous loss. It substitutes the past for the

[1] Heb. v. 7.　　　　[2] Heb. iv. 14, 15.

present, the historic Jesus for the living Christ. Of course, the historic fact holds its essential place. But the spiritual reality of redemption is going on now. At this very hour Christ is engaged in heaven in the spirit of reparation.

III

We now pass to our final theme, which is the Church's Offering on Earth.

Now, clearly, the character of the Church's devotion on earth is determined by the attitude of our Lord in Heaven. The Church's devotion must correspond with the devotion of Christ. What Christ does there, the Church must do here. If Christ is perpetually absorbed in the redemptive offering, in the spirit of reparation, in propitiation there in Heaven, the Church must be similarly occupied here on earth.

1. Consider the first Eucharist. Think of the language employed. Christ, when He took the chalice, said, 'This is My Blood of the Covenant.' In the modern mind these terms awake but a languid interest. They sound remote and obsolete. But Christ was not primarily addressing us. He was speaking to Jews. And to the Jew those terms were alive with historical associations. They were so many allusions to the worship of Israel, perfectly clear and illuminating to a Jew, conveying very definite conceptions indeed. They would recall the historic scene when Moses completed the union between God and Israel, inaugurated a new offering, and exclaimed, 'This is the Blood of the Covenant.' Christ's hearers

could not fail to understand, in the light of this deliberate historic parallel, that He was effecting a union between God and mankind, a new reconciliation between Heaven and earth, and that this Blood of the Covenant was the offering by which that union was secured. This Blood of the Covenant was not intended merely to remind themselves : it was a reminder before God. It was no mere dramatic appeal to the imaginations of men; it was a Godward appeal, directed in prayer and offering to the Father.

We have looked at that first Eucharist from the side of the Apostles ; let us look at it also from the side of Christ. He instituted the Eucharist at an hour which might well appear most inappropriate. For it was an hour of strain and suspense, when anything like calm concentration and reflection must have been for the disciples immeasurably more difficult than if the Institution had been far away from Jerusalem, in some quiet corner of the Holy Land. But it is impossible not to see the supreme significance of the hour which was chosen. Christ set the first Eucharist as close as possible to His death. He was Himself the Celebrant. His mind was full of anticipation. He was dwelling in His Passion. It appears in His conversation, in His acts, in His whole demeanour, in His prayer, in everything. The time was only an hour or two before Gethsemane. Is it possible to doubt that He was already offering the Blood of the Covenant to the Father in heaven ; that the great Propitiation was begun ; that the first Eucharist, with Christ as the visible Celebrant, was part and parcel of the great process by which the world was redeemed; that the spirit of reparation was expressed all through His actions and His utterances?

2. Does not the same hold true of every Eucharist since?

The present Bishop of Durham said some years ago: 'I believe that if our eyes . . . were open to the unseen, we should indeed behold our Lord present at our Communions. . . . Such special presence . . . is properly mysterious in mode, but absolutely true in fact; no creation of our imagination or emotion, but an object for our faith. I believe that our Lord so present . . . would be seen Himself, in our presence, to bless the bread and wine for a holy use, and to distribute them to His disciples.'[1]

These are remarkable words. But in reality they imply still more. For if Christ is still the true Celebrant, He is present in the spirit of reparation, in the spirit of intercession, in the purpose of perpetual self-offering before the Father which is characteristic of Him in His ascended state. He continues to do in every Eucharist what He did in the earliest Eucharist of all. This is the justification of the well-known hymn which has become endeared by the most sacred devotional experience to multitudes:

> And now, O Father, mindful of the love
>   That bought us, once for all, on Calvary's Tree,
> And having with us Him that pleads above,
>   We here present, we here spread forth to Thee
> That only Offering perfect in Thine eyes,
> The one true, pure, immortal Sacrifice.

[1] *Report of Conference held at Fulham Palace*, 1900, p. 72.

THE PERPETUAL OFFERING OF CHRIST

IV

We have contemplated three great subjects: Christ's Offering on the Cross, Christ's Offering in Heaven, the Church's Offering on earth. If they are to be rightly understood, they must be considered together. For they are intimately related. They are parts of one vast whole. The reason why people do not believe in the eucharistic offering is because they have no belief in the heavenly offering of Christ. And they have no belief in the heavenly offering of Christ because they think of redemption rather as an act than as a spirit, a solitary deed rather than a moral attitude. Could we but look beyond the outward expression to the inward state, we should surely acknowledge that Christ's offering is the offering of His inmost Self, and therefore must be an offering in perpetuity. And then half our controversies about redemption would be at an end. We could be absorbed in that consummation so devoutly to be desired, when disputations cease and devotion begins.

PRINTED BY
SPOTTISWOODE AND CO. LTD., COLCHESTER
LONDON AND ETON

DATE DUE

DATE DUE			
NOV 0 8 1997			